ENERGIES IN MY BODY...

... *The Greatest Blessings Of My Life!!!*

To you...

With all my Love...

Copyright © 2016 by Soul T Alma ™

ISBN: 978-0-9969-6670-2

Other Creations

Books

- **Energías En Mi Cuerpo... ¡¡¡Las Bendiciones Más Grandes De Mi Vida!!!**
- **Running Out Of Time... Is That Even Possible???**

- **Se Me Acaba El Tiempo... ¿¿¿De Verdad Crees Que Eso Es Posible???**
- **More... Life-Changing... Life-Giving... Never-Ending... TOUGHTS...**
- **Más… PENSAMIENTOS… Transformadores… Que-Dan-Vida… Que-Nunca-Terminan…**
- **A FRIEND I Didn't Know I Had…**
- **UNA AMISTAD Que No Sabía Que Tenía...**

Websites
soultalma.com

Contact Information
Email Address: SoulTAlma@yahoo.com

Contents

Do not think about page numbers or anything else... You will get there... Wherever "there" is... If and when it is the right time for you... All in perfect timing... Like they say... No worries... Only Joy!!!

Chapter 1-- **AMAZEMENT**- Before And... After?

Chapter 2-- **ENERGIES** In My Body

Chapter 3-- January 7th, 2013: **THE TURNING POINT**

Chapter 4-- And **THE VOYAGE TO THE "CENTER OF ME"** Began

Chapter 5-- The Eagerness... Or The Need... **TO WRITE**

Chapter 6-- The Way I Am **NOW**

Chapter 7-- The "Theory" Of **GETTING OUT OF FOCUS**

Chapter 8-- If This Isn't **ABUNDANCE...** Then What Is It?

Chapter 9-- **ABUNDANCE...** A Bottomless Pit Of **BLESSINGS** And **MIRACLES...**

Chapter 10-- From The Universe **TO ME** And **FROM ME** To The Universe

Chapter 11-- **WHERE TO** Now???

11:11-- Epilogue

Chapter 1-- AMAZEMENT- Before And... After?

It is so amazing to witness everything that has happened to me... It is something beyond miraculous... All the things people usually spend a lifetime trying to find... To feel... To live... From the smallest... Simplest details... To the greatest things... All of them have come to me without me even trying to find them or looking for them...

Could it be that this saying I have heard so many times during the past few years... That of "it is all inside of you" ... Is true? ... Could it be that one doesn't actually have to go anywhere to find all the Joy... The blessings... The miracles in life? ...

It has to be true because... Honestly... I have not done anything to try to find anything... It all has shown to me… It all has "appeared" as if by magic…

Now that I have spent over two years "going through this" … I find it to be the most normal thing in the world… Somehow I kind of expect it… And this is a miracle all in itself because I had spent the first 42 years of my life being the most "fatalistic" … Fearful… Low-deserving… Low self-esteemed person you could ever meet…

Now… After having been very used to this "magic" for the past two years… And realizing that now all this "magic" is the most normal thing in the world to me…

Now… When I spend more than a few seconds thinking about it… When I start to realize about the magnitude and depth of all of this… And start to think about how difficult (rare) it is that these things actually happen… And then… The longer I think about it that way... The more I start to wonder why are these things happening to me so easily... And... "Who am I" to deserve all of this... And then I quickly feel that if I continue letting my thoughts go in that direction... I easily end up in the same low self-esteem... Lack of self-worth... Etc... All of that negativity that used to be the main trait of my personality before... And yes... It has been a very gradual process... And I see that before I used to easily end up in that low-deserving trap...

Oh but now.... Now I gradually have been able to catch myself faster... And have been able to pull myself out of it sooner... To the point that now it is very uncomfortable to feel that type of negativity in me... Even for a few seconds... Now it is much easier... And much more natural for me... To expect all kinds of blessings to happen inside of me and around me all the time :) ...

I guess the fact that I had lived my life in lack of self-appreciation… Self-love… And self-worth… I have not thought I actually deserved much… Instead, I have just stumbled through life… Realizing about the things I did not like… And moving on from there to something else… Realizing how much I did not want that either… And then moving on to something else… And to something else… So I became an expert at "the things I did not like or did not want to experience" … I became an expert at not wanting anything… At thinking that I did not deserve anything… At thinking that I needed to train myself to not want anything... So then I would not feel disappointed about anything…

And then little but surely I became numb… My mind became numb… My feelings became numb… My body became almost paralyzed… My emotions became an obscure abyss in which I buried every thought… Every idea… Every

dream... And the worst... I became so used to it!
...

So much so that I got to the point of not even realizing that this was not normal at all... That it did not have to be that way... I got to the point of thinking at first... And being very convinced as the years went by... That there was nothing in this world for me... Not understanding the meaning of anything... Not finding sense or purpose in anything... Especially in me...

All the first 42 years of my life went like this... I realized that I did not like THAT (whatever THAT was)... And moved on from there to something else... And every time what I was moving to was something less liked by me... And less wanted... And less appealing... And my life was somewhat of a slowly-but-surely-down-the-hill-ride year after year... Day after day... Minute after minute... Everything... My studies... My career… My relationships… My self-worth… My body weight… My body image… My blood pressure… My personality… My emotions… Etc… Etc… Everything in my life went down that same path…

And I could not understand… And no one at least somewhat close to me could understand… WHY????? … Why someone like me?????? … Why someone with such loving family… Loving friends… Loving teachers… "Beautiful life"? … Why someone so smart… So intelligent… And yes… Even so pretty? … Why me… Having "everything in the world?" … Why other people… Who lived in real tough situations… Seemed to be so happy??? … And… Here I was… Following this unstoppable down-the-hill journey… WHY??????

Something very powerful happened to me one day in January of 2013… That "something" caused... Or... Better yet... Helped me to at least stop... No... It would be much more accurate to say... "Somewhat slow down" ... The down-the-hill motion of my life... The lack of direction in my life... The low self-esteem... At least it helped me to somehow realize that I could hit the brake pedal to slow down that kind of motion... To bring that negative motion to a lower speed... To at least be able to realize... To assess... How delicate my situation was... To slow down and actually be able to look around with a little bit less blurriness... To slow down and at least be sometimes able to breathe in a meaningful way... To slow down and be able to realize how fast my thoughts were constantly going down that negative path... To slow down and start sometimes... Even if only for a matter of seconds... To just BE... Yes... To just BE...

At that time I suddenly realized how exhausted I was... How exhausted my body was...

How exhausted my mind was… How exhausted my feelings were… How exhausted my Soul and my Spirit were... How much confusion there was in my Being… How much lack of understanding there was in my Being… How many contradictions had accumulated in my Being throughout the first 42 years of my life…

I... Somehow… Do not even know how… Reached somewhat of a plateau after that… A "plateau" that should not be called "that" because it was not peaceful or stable at all… It was a "plateau" just on the surface… But in the inside there was a combination of constant avalanches… Tsunamis… Earthquakes… Volcanoes… Tornadoes… Hurricanes… And everything else imaginable along those lines :) …

The intense… Confusing… Unbearable energies started within myself… The intense "going within" started to happen inside of me…

The intense and unstoppable impulses to reflect and remember and re-assess my life started to happen inside of me… The intense writings started to build up inside of me… To the point that I had to give up every time… Stop everything I had to do… And just write… And write… And write…

Intense feelings started to increase exponentially inside of me… Many feelings that I had never even experienced before or imagined that existed… All of this made me feel and realize that my life… My whole life… Had been a total contradiction up to that point… A total lack of direction up to that point… A total confusion up to that point… Full of things that I had wanted at some point… And then gave up on them because of my lack of direction… My lack of knowing how worthy I am… My lack of Love…

I am delighted at the way I have been feeling after that… And I am even more delighted to realize that this beautiful state of Being has lasted pretty steadily all this time… I have experienced a slowly-but-surely-up-the-hill-motion in my life now… This is so calming… So relieving!!! … So much so that I want it to last forever and ever!!! …

I can tell you… There hasn't been a time in my life where I have felt like this… It is a feeling… So beautiful and so strange at the same time… A feeling that something inside of me is moving up up up and bubbling… Like a hot spring… But sometimes… Many times… Instead of "that something" moving up and up… Slowly bubbling from inside of me… It shoots out like a geyser… It would probably be more accurate to describe it as a "bubbling geyser" … Yes… That is actually perfect for how I have felt these past couple of years of my life :) …

But… Wait a minute!!! … What is "that something" that moves like a "bubbling geyser" from inside of me??? … What is it? … At first I felt it was like a "foreign object" … Something that "was placed" inside of me all of a sudden… And was finding its way out…

But as the days… The months… Even the years went by… As I embraced this process more and more… As I embraced it like my last resort… As I was able to sense… To truly feel what was happening inside of me… In all that process I realized that it was not a "foreign object" … That nothing was placed inside of me… That it all had been there all along… It was parts of me that were emerging like a "bubbling geyser" … It was Me… It was My Being… My True Self… What a lovely… Delightful… What a magical experience!!!!!!

One day... Reading some of the writings that I had started... So many of them! ... To see which one I wanted to continue... I suddenly realized that the first 42 years of my life I have had it all backwards...

Yes... I innately did not like conflict... And I always had the tendency to just let things happen... And when something displeasing happened to me... Or when some wrongdoing was done to me... I basically let it all be... Without fighting back or anything...

And yes... I now realize that it was probably the best thing to do because going against things just basically adds more fuel to the fire, per se... But I never realized that this was happening because something inside of me was "causing" it...

So instead of being able to remediate the situation... And do something so it would not happen again… Event after event… Action after action… I just took more and more on a path of less and less self-worthiness… As if for some reason I deserved all these "negative" things happening to me…

And moment after moment… Year after year… More and more lack of self-esteem… More and more lack of self-love… Going down this hill that became steeper and steeper every time… In every area of my life… And the hill got steeper because the increase of those negative feelings toward myself grew deeper and deeper as the years and the experiences passed by…

Chapter 2-- ENERGIES In My Body

It is very curious to me to remember that I was always a very indecisive person… Very insecure… Always needing support from others… Always calling everyone so I wouldn't feel alone… Looking for protection… For understanding… Always asking others before I could make any decision… Even if a very small decision… Asking anyone around me… Especially my closest family members and friends… I was famous for that… Everyone… Including me… Were all so used to that… So much so that we accepted it as the most normal thing in the world…

And to see me now going through all these energies and all these "strange" things… All those things that at the beginning used to make me think that I was going out of my mind… Or that perhaps I was getting sick or something very bad was happening in my body... To see me going through all of that and that I never had the intention to call anyone or tell what was happening... It's as if a miracle had taken place in me...

And yes... Looking at it now from the distance... And reflecting on everything that has happened to me since all of that began... I KNOW that is what happened... I Know that a miracle happened in me... It is as if from the very beginning I had something like a trust... Despite the total confusion... An internal trust that told me that everything was fine... A profound Knowing that this was... And is... Something that I had to go through alone...

And perhaps that is why at the moment that everything was going to start... In that precise and magical moment... They put THAT BEING in front of me... Through many coincidences and through ITS energy... In an instant... Very abruptly... Or maybe it was the sudden closeness to THAT BEING what caused all this process to unleash and accelerate itself inside of me? ... Or could it be that it was all destined to take place at the same time? ...

I do not know... The only thing I Know is that this is the most beautiful thing that has ever happened in my life... And it is very amazing to me that now... Remembering the "beginning" of all of this... And the moments when I was living it... Without knowing what it was... Now I realize that I always felt that if this same process would happen to many other people I know... That if this would happen to at least 90% of the people that currently inhabit this planet... That if this same thing would have happened to me in some previous moment of my life...

They (and I) would rush to see a doctor... Be it a doctor of the body or the mind... And they would start to receive treatment for this or the other… And from there, something very similar to a chain reaction would start to happen… Where from one thing they would find another… And another… And the first medication would cause other problems that they would try to treat later with other medications… And so forth and so on…

No! … That thought never even occurred to me… Could it be that this happened precisely to me because I have always been the type of person that would only go to doctors in a very extreme circumstance? … Or perhaps this has happened… And happens… To many other people… But because they have the tendency to "fix" things through medications… Surgeries… Treatments for this or for that… Somehow they slowly "annihilate" … Or "mask" … Or "severe" the process… And they do not allow this which started to happen, to develop and continue its natural course? … And would it be that… Precisely for my way of acting... I was a "fertile medium" for all of this to develop little by little in me? ...

My tendency was to just observe it and flow with the current... Sometimes astonished... Exhausted others... Always impressed... Confused most of the time... But always with that sensation... With something very subtle and imperceptible that was guiding me and telling me that everything was fine...

And I even think that perhaps the fact that all the first 42 years of my life I was so insecure... So indecisive... I had such low self-esteem... So little, almost non-existent, self-love... I used to assign such little value to myself... That in that time... And along all those previous years... I used to allow everything to happen to me without complaining... Without doing anything about it... Without realizing that things did not have to be that way...

Would it be that… Precisely because of all of that I allowed all of this to happen without asking anyone… Without telling anyone… Without going to anyone to try to receive help??? … Could it be that being like that has acted as a survival mechanism for me during all the first 42 years of my life? … I do not know… I will never be able to know with certainty…

The first times that I started to receive those "energy cycles" … "Coincidentally" right after THAT BEING "was put" in my life… Just like that… So abruptly… Those extremely intense "energy cycles" … So baffling… So overwhelming… So leveling and unstoppable… I started to realize that after everything was "over" the result was always something beautiful… Something positive… Some type of beneficial change in me…

Eventually the doubts dissipated in me… Little by little… The confusion dissipated in me… And every time "that" happened in me, I Knew it was another one of those miraculous cycles… Those cycles that even when they many times left me with my body almost devastated … With my mind totally exhausted… As if they had turned me inside out…

I Knew it was for something good… And I used to go through them with inner happiness… "Observing me" each time with greater pleasure… With more satisfaction… With deeper trust…

Each time what I received after all those extremely intense energies traveled through my Spirit… Through my Soul… Through my body… Throughout my whole Being… Is something to which I cannot give any other name than "A Blessing" … In my body… In my personality…

More and more joy… More and more mental clarity…

The first years it was something pretty constant and extremely intense… Now… This third year those "energy cycles" have become a little more spaced out… A little less intense maybe… The energies a little more calmed… Not always uniquely related to THAT BEING… The same process has occurred to me with a couple of other people and a few other things also…

And now as I write this I ask myself… Could it be that it is not that the cycles are more spaced out… Or the energies less intense… But that my Being has adapted to all of this… And that this is part of who I am now… And I do not see them as something strange, but as the most normal things in the world to me? …

I do not know... All I know is that I miss the confusion I felt in those days... The "shocks" ... The "agonies" and the "fears" I felt at the beginning... The intensity... The way I used to see and Feel miracles... Big and small... Take place in me every day... Many times several times in the same day...

I wish that each person that goes through this process is able to realize right away of the huge blessing they are receiving in their Being... And just enjoy every instant... As "baffling" as it may be...

Yes... My body received many blessings during that time... VERY MANY!!!! ... Among them... Many that I will never tell anyone... The most "perceivable" ones of these blessings... Some perceivable by other people... Others only perceivable by me... Those perceivable blessings are...

The total disappearance of my obesity... Something that I suffered from during the previous thirteen years to when all this started... *The total disappearance of my high blood pressure...* And not taking pills and being always normal... Something that I suffered from during the previous seven years to when all this started... *The total disappearance of certain pains...* From the very beginning of all this starting to happen... Something that I suffered from religiously from the very first time... Every month during the previous thirty one years to when all this started... *The total disappearance of my breathing problems... The miraculous increase of my flexibility and elasticity...*

And there was a point when I just decided to accept the fact that the *arthritis*... And not being able to use my knees for anything... Not being able to bend them even the slightest... Was going to be the price that I had to pay for all those years of my obesity… For all those years of so many other things that lead me to that obesity… And to that arthritis…

But… The same… Many people used to tell me that I was going to have to go to a doctor to at least have them check me… And I was totally reluctant because then they would find this or the other… And then they would want me to undergo surgery to replace my knees… Which is what I saw them doing to most people…

And I continued living my life normally… I bought supplements that perhaps would help me to improve this condition… And I continued to go to my exercises… And it was very… Very painful for me… And many times I used to cry from so much pain… The intense pain in my knees used to wake me up in the middle of the night after doing the exercises…

And one day I had a feeling while I was in my bed... In that "limbo" state as I was falling asleep... And it was a sensation that even if I had that situation going on with my knees... Even in that situation... I was going to live happily...

And many more months passed by... Living my life... Living happily in my pain... And about three months ago I started to notice that the pain had disappeared... But I did not want to totally convince myself... Just in case... And I would observe me once in a while... Pretending I wasn't really paying attention to this :) ...

And yes... Today I can categorically say that my knees are totally fine... With such flexibility I don't believe I ever had in my life... Not even when I was young... What name could I assign to this... Other than "A Blessing?" :) ...

Yes... My personality received many blessings also... As the years in my life went by I became... At first very slowly and very gradually... And then very rapidly... Someone that was always sad... Apathetic... Disinterested... I used to always be a fairly happy person... I liked to laugh... I used to love to listen to music... Visit new places... And during the twelve years prior to all of this beginning to happen a very noticeable change took place in me... It all came to a point where I would never smile... I used to live without ever listening to music... Always upset about one thing or another...

From the moment when all this started to happen to me I transformed myself very abruptly... If we compare it to the previous years of my life... And especially the last twelve... In a happy person... In such an instantaneous way... As if a "fairy godmother" had touched me with her magic wand or something similar to that...

I went from the total depression in which I had lived practically all my life… To be always happy… Always full of life… I went from being the least motivated person that has ever existed on this planet… To being always eager… Full of enthusiasm… I went from being the introverted person I had been all my life… To being a very spontaneous and fairly open person… From being a very indecisive person… Without a clear direction in life… To being someone with acute mental clarity… Totally sure of myself…

Yes… My spirituality received many blessings… I would say that around turning ten years of age… I started to have very specific ideas about many things… About many topics that are not what one would see as "children's topics" … And it was as if I had a very deep inner understanding about all these things that I thought… Or no… Not only that I "thought" … It would be more accurate to say that I Knew… About the majority of the most important aspects of a Human Being's life…

How did I acquire that knowledge and reach those conclusions about Life at such a young age? … I do not know… Perhaps due to many aspects related to the first ten years of my existence… Related to my upbringing… With things I used to observe in others… With things I used to hear… I am not sure…

What I am certain about is that at that young age I realized that the majority of those things that I thought… Or that I Knew… The majority of the aspects of my personality… My way of being… What I used to expect from life and from others… Did not match at all with what I saw around me… It did not match at all with the way I used to see the people around me talk, act, think…

And just like that… Little by little… I started to feel strange in this world… To the point that I became very deeply convinced that I did not belong in this world at all… So… In that state of being I lived the thirty two years prior to the moment when all this started to happen… And here I do not include the first ten years of my life because I do not remember much of what I used to feel back then…

But what I know is that when I was between six months and one year of going through this process… I suddenly realized that I was not feeling none of that "strangeness" … I realized that… Even though I still felt different than the majority of the people in many… Many aspects… Interests… Way of being… Way of behaving… Way of seeing life… Etc… There would never be anyone or anything able to make me feel that I do not belong in this world…

And I see the world… Life… Everything… With so much beauty… Everything makes sense… Everything has meaning… Everything… Everything that has happened to me in my life makes total sense… So many "knowings" … So many understandings have "downloaded" … And continue to "download" themselves in me… Just like that… In an instant… Without me looking for them… Without me expecting them…

Yes… My actions received many blessings… My way of behaving has changed so much… In such an incredible way! … After all this started to happen a little over two years ago…

The closest people to me… The ones that had to suffer the consequences of all my depressions… Negativities… Sadnesses… Low self-esteem… And everything I have mentioned before… Are the most amazed ones to see how much I have changed… So "abruptly" …

Even I am totally amazed by all of this… Despite the fact that I have been the main witness of every little change… Of every second in which I felt something relax itself inside of me… Similar to a valve that was causing tension in certain area of my existence… And all of a sudden the valve opens up and everything flows again…

At the beginning everyone… Including me… Thought it was going to be just a fleeting event… As if I was just suddenly having some "clarity moments" that would then return to the "obscure" normal state in which I had lived up to that point in my life…

And this is something totally understandable… First, there is that of "if it is too good to be true, it probably isn't true" … There are others' expectations, which are generally based on the history of what has happened up to that moment…

And when one thinks that a person has been a certain way… In a very stable manner… During the first 42 years of that person's life… It is impossible to think that such a drastic change is going to occur overnight… So "from its roots all the way up" … So "from the deepest essence" … And that it is going to be something permanent…

In fact, I have spent all my life… Literally… Trying to change… Trying with more intensity the more I realized that the intensity of my "not belonging" … The intensity of my depression… The intensity of my sadness… The intensity of my unhappiness… The more I realized that the intensity was increasing…

And at the end I never accomplished much… Some relief… Some temporary improvement to then go back to the same… Or… Not really to "the same" … To something much more negative and much more disconnected every time…

Chapter 3-- January 7th, 2013: THE TURNING POINT

"That day" of January of 2013 I went to the Supermarket close to my mom's house... A quick... Usual trip to just buy some milk... Bananas... And a couple of other everyday items... That Supermarket is just two or three blocks from her house... On a road that I drive almost every day... Sometimes even two or three times a day...

As I was driving back to my mom's house... Suddenly I started to see everything so beautiful... Something truly "out of this world" ... And yet, it was the same street... The same trees... The same sun... The same sky... The same houses that I was so used to seeing every day... Many times several times a day...

And even though everything was the same... I was sure everything was the same... I was not dreaming or anything! ... I was driving! ... How was it possible that such an "invasion" of beauty suddenly came to my life? ...

It wasn't that things appeared to be a different color... No... Same colors... But it was as if they had a different tone... A different glow... Not quite a shine... Just like a glow... Just as if they were more blended one into the other... As if the boundaries had somehow faded... As if everything was just a continuum of everything else... Such beauty! ... Such Love!!! ... Love? ...

Yes!!! ... That is exactly... Or at least as closely as I can describe it... That is what I felt slowly inundating my whole body... Little by little... Pore by pore... So beautiful! ... Such a feeling of deep, intense, infinite Love!!! ... I really feel even the word Love is not accurate to describe something so pure and so magnificent... In every tree... In the sky... In every home... In every car... Inside my car... Inside of me... In every millimeter of my body... Of my Soul... And my heart? ...

My heart was about to explode... It was the first time I felt this... My whole chest area was about to explode... The closest I can describe it is as if suddenly all that area became something very similar to a balloon... And it kept expanding and expanding... And I clearly and very deeply felt all that huge space within myself... As if it was filled with air... But... No!... It did not feel like air! ... How could I describe that feeling???? ...

It was Love...

All of a sudden I was filled with Love... Totally bathing me on the inside... On the outside... All around me... But... What is this????

... Where does all of this come from???? ... This is so beautiful!!!! ... I have never seen or felt or sensed something so absolutely beautiful... What is it? ... What is it? ...

Those were my thoughts in the middle of all that awe and deep admiration... When I suddenly stopped myself and said "I do not know what it is... Or where it comes from... All I want to do is enjoy it and assimilate it" ...

So much beauty!!! ... So much Love!!! ... It feels like it lasted an eternity... As if everything had slowed down or stopped... Just for me to enjoy... But I know it was just a matter of seconds because I was already in my mom's parking place...

And I clearly remember me standing in my mom's kitchen once I got in her house and telling her... "Mom, I do not know why... Or when... Or how… But I know that from this moment on I will not be the same person ever again" …

And then she started asking me… "But what do you mean? … But what happened? … But why do you say that?" … To which I could only say every time… "I do not know mom… Don't ask me… I just sense it" …

And then I described to her everything that had happened to me seconds ago… And all she could say was… "That was strange!" …

All of a sudden... Two days later... I had the impulse to start communicating with "THAT BEING" … It was as if… Out of the blue… Something pushed me to communicate with IT …

Honestly… At the beginning I did not even know why I was doing that… After so many years… All those years it was as if somehow I constantly had ITS presence in me… But did not feel the need… The purpose… Or the sense… To communicate with IT… So I had no clue on what to say… But I kept feeling "that push" … That undeniable push to reach out and communicate…

One day… One afternoon… Two days after that push to communicate began… Four days after that "magical experience" happened to me on my way to my mom's house… As I was writing… Working… Studying at my desk… Perhaps somewhat thinking about THAT BEING… Perhaps… I am not sure… I cannot remember…

All I clearly remember is that I was sitting at my desk… Just sitting at my desk… And very unexpectedly I felt a presence standing behind me… Very clearly I felt THIS BEING standing behind me… In such an intense manner that I turned toward my left side saying ITS name aloud… "-----???" …

And it was very "saddening" … Very "empty feeling" … Not sure what word to use to describe it… But I felt very amazed to see THIS BEING was not there… No One was there… But I felt IT standing there behind me… I felt IT… What was it? … ITS energy? …

Chapter 4-- And **THE VOYAGE TO THE "CENTER OF ME" Began**

I had always been the most fearful person that probably exists… I never wanted to be alone… Even as an adult… All my life I was always with somebody… First… In my parents' home… Then in the dorms at school… Then in my marriage…

Eventually I ended up in jobs where I had to work at the computer a lot… And I had to work a lot… And my work hours extended pretty much throughout the whole day… Night… Weekends… It ended up being almost 24/7…

So the time of the day came when everyone had to go to bed… And I did not want to stay all by myself in the dining room or in a bedroom that used to function as "my office/guest room" … I remember me gathering my laptops… My little portable desk… And sticking all of that... Plus me with a chair... Inside the master bathroom… So I would stay close to my spouse… But not close enough as to have to turn on the lights in the bedroom…

I remember me going through things like that all my life… And my close relatives and friends had to suffer the consequences of my behaviors... Of my imbalance… Again... Not really sure what name to give it…

And it was something so constant in me that they… And I… Were so used to it… And even though we knew it was not normal… We gave up after years and years of trying and trying unsuccessfully to change me…

And… Like this example I describe… The rest of the examples of my restless… Unbalanced personality during the first 42 years of my life are just endless… And it doesn't truly make sense to spend any more time describing them here…

I just wanted to somehow illustrate this… So it is easier to understand the significance that this drastic change had for me… To the point that I consider it also a miracle… Another one of the many… Countless miracles that started to happen to me after "that day" in January of 2013…

After what happened to me on "that day"… And after my first communication with THAT BEING, that started two days later… I automatically had the urge… The impulse… To start waking up somewhere between 1:00 a.m. and

3:00 a.m. … Every day… And quietly and in a very relaxed way… Go outside the bedroom area… Head to the kitchen… Make coffee… Or whatever was appealing to me that day… Do a couple of stretching exercises while the coffee was done… And then head to "my office/guest-room area" … And there spend the next several hours all by myself… So relaxed… In such communion with me… In such depth of Being…

I am not sure how to explain it… I just know that it felt so wonderful… So natural… So nurturing… That I became more and more eager to do it every day… So good that even today… Around two-and -a half years after all this started to happen to me… I still eagerly do that every day of my life… Even though many of my life circumstances have drastically changed since then…

Every day... For at least the first year... I would meditate very deeply... Something I had started on and off during the 8 years prior to 2013... And that I started doing very specifically and constantly during 2012... Increasing the intensity in the last two months of that year...

Before 2012, I did not really know what I was doing... I just had a sense that I had to do something... Something to feel better... As I said... All my life I have tried not to be depressed... To increase my self-esteem... Etc... Etc... But that is another story...

So... A few months after all this started in 2013 I would meditate... Then I would start to either read things on the Internet... Or listen to different people in Youtube... Or listen to different songs that would suddenly pop in my head... And would make me reflect on certain things... Or bring me different memories of my life... Or make me reflect on different things from different times of my life...

Many times I would communicate with THAT BEING about the different things that were triggered by my reflections... And the things THAT BEING said... Or didn't say... Would trigger something else in me... A deeper reflection... A deeper understanding... A "letting go" of something... Many... Many things would start to quickly be built up in me... Thoughts... Feelings... Energy... Many physical sensations... Very uncomfortable... Very strange... Things I had never felt before... Things that would trigger even more things in me...

More reflections... More Knowings... More understandings... More communications with THIS BEING... Until everything came to a point where the only thing I could do was to write... And write... And write... A letter...

A letter that was written from the new standpoint that I had acquired after the deep… Abrupt Knowings that came to me in the first two weeks of this process going on with me… And the answer I received from THIS BEING when still in the middle of reading my letter…

That response triggered something that had NEVER, EVER happened to me in my whole entire existence… Feelings that had never happened to me… And that I was always "sure" they could not exist… Not in the world I had perceived and lived in up to that point…

But somehow I knew they did exist… And perhaps that was at the essence of all the contradictions and deep discordance I had experienced all my life…

THAT BEING'S response triggered all these energies to unleash within me… This response triggered a more intense and deeper than ever "going within" … The response of THIS BEING triggered something so unique and so intense!!! …

All of this happened in such "symphony-like" fashion… Like in a perfect sequence of events… In perfect timing…

See… If THIS BEING had appeared in my life… In this way… In any of the prior 42 years, right up to "that day" in January of 2013… I would have quickly and skillfully blocked and eliminated ITS presence from my life completely… None of this that happened at the beginning of January and all the beautiful things… Blessings… And miracles that happened after that… None of them would have taken place at all…

So… I am not sure if that wonderful… That "out of this world" experience that happened to me "that day" of January of 2013… As I was driving to my mom's house… And the first two events that happened about THIS BEING the second and fourth day after that… Made me just flow with it and let things be… To see what this was all about… Thinking I was receiving some signs and perhaps THIS BEING needed some type of help from me…

And then that "strong pull" that was happening right from the beginning… And then all the amazing and beautiful synchronicities that started to take place… THIS BEING's responses to me… My reactions… My going deeper… My total opening… My going even deeper within myself… All the feelings inside of me… My amazement… More feelings… Feelings that were totally unknown to me… And that pull… That irresistible pull! … This time it was absolutely irresistible…

I was so paralyzed in amazement to see myself allowing me to follow all of this… To receive whatever was coming my way… Puzzled by the way everything was happening… Puzzled by what was happening… Astonished by how fast and how deeply everything was taking place… So deeply that all of this was reaching the innermost core layer of my Being… Transforming me from my very core… From the very essence of who I truly was…

This was the first time ever that I actually allowed myself to flow with Life… Without me rigidly controlling every bit of what was entering my life… Like I had always done… Always rigidly micromanaging everything from a very negative… Contradictory… And confused standpoint…

Perhaps all the conditions around THIS BEING… So real… But at the same time almost like in the spiritual world… The specific circumstances that somehow linked us… All of this made me not to push IT away from me from the very beginning… I was distracted thinking this was all about something else…

And when I realized what was truly happening inside of me related to THIS BEING… I had already gone too far… And was in the middle of the strongest pull I have ever experienced in my whole life…

Chapter 5-- The Eagerness... Or The Need... TO WRITE

I have been feeling those happy energies so much these couple of days... Much more intense than usual... And usually... For the past two years... My normal state is like what for at least 90% of people would be a very heightened... Excited... Upbeat state...

So when I feel in this state that I am currently feeling... Which I have felt many... Many times before for the past two years... A state that I have come to identify with and understand so deeply...

When I feel in this extra-charged… Super-happy state… One of the descriptions that comes to my mind… Probably the only description that comes to my mind… Is that my body is about to explode… I literally feel that way… I just mentioned it to a friend of mine… And she looked at me like I am out of my mind…

Another way to describe it would be like my skin cannot hold me anymore… Like when you inflate a balloon… That is exactly how my body feels in the periods where I feel this intense… Beautiful… All encompassing energy…

And I literally feel that I need to find ways to calm it down a little because… Like a balloon… If you put a little too much air in it… In a sudden way… It explodes… Or if the material of the balloon is not in 100% … Optimal condition… It cannot hold much either…

In those moments of such intense energy nothing helps much… It is something much more powerful than my mind and my body… And I am not sure where it comes from… It happens "just like that" … "Out of the blue" …

And since I do not have intentions to go from this world yet… When I get to that point of feeling that "That's it! … I cannot hold anymore or my body explodes" … When I get to that point I do different things to try to at least calm the energies down… And I have found a handful of things that work for me…

Closing my eyes and relaxing my body a little… Taking deep... Slow breaths down to my belly… Slow enough to feel how the air slowly reaches every place inside my body… Closing my eyes and imagining that I am inside the ocean… The whole ocean just for me :) ... Or in a river… Only for me :) … Or under a slow flowing waterfall… And especially… Drinking water as if I had spent a week lost in the desert… Among others…

But… Like I said… These are just helpful to distract me in that peak moment when my body literally cannot hold anymore… And it is "about to explode" … Just as a minor relief… It would not even make sense for me to do it the rest of the time…

Up to this point I had always related those energies with THAT BEING… Always sensing and knowing that I did not have anything to do with this because everything came and started from outside of me… Almost as if it was something totally imposed on me…

But since for the past two years we have been somewhat close… I always thought all this was directly… Uniquely related to THIS BEING's presence in my life… And could never understand why someone that I didn't even know that much… Why someone that was very… Very far from me in every kind of imaginable way… Why "that someone" would make me feel all these things that I had never felt in all the years of my life put together…

These past several months THIS BEING has been very distant… And now… The last few days… These intense energies again… Very intense… What causes them? … Not sure what causes them… I am only sure that it is the same that caused them the very first time… And all the other times after that…

Something happened in my life from the very beginning all this started… A little over two years ago… In relation to THIS BEING… Since IT was brought to me at the very same instant all this began to happen… Very simultaneously… All of it in a very sudden and abrupt manner… So all these years this almost magical thing happened to me… The need to write… And write… And write… To THIS BEING…

Knowing that all of that does not originate in me… Trying to stop it before it even starts… But my body literally fills up… And I literally feel something stuck inside of me… Something that fills my whole body… From my lower belly all the way to my throat… Something that burns me from the inside…

All the exact ideas and words and phrases are inside of me… Filling me up… And the more I resist… The more full I feel… And the more I cannot even think of anything else… The more I am pushed to sit down and write…

But I do not want to do it because it literally takes up all my energy… All my time… All my thoughts… All of me… And I know that I need to do all the things I need to do in my day… I cannot just neglect everything, everyone, and me, and just write and write and write…

Those are my thoughts when I am trying not to give in to it… But the moment comes when it is just so much! … So much that I have no other choice but to sit down and do it…

Hours and hours writing… Sometimes it takes me a couple of days to finish because of the obligations I need to tend to in between… And during all that time I am completely taken by all of this… Most of the times I write from around 2:00 a.m. to around 7:00 a.m. … That is a block of time where I do not have any interruptions…

The times when there have not been interruptions… And I have been able to sit down and continue beyond 7:00 am… And finish…

After many many hours non-stop… My fingers and my whole hand hurt… My fingers are red and feel literally burned from so much writing…

During all the process before I sit down… Plus all the hours of writing… A unique and hugely intense energy travels through my body and burns me from the inside out…

Sometimes I am thinking the writing is going one way… And what ends up being "on paper" is totally different… At some point I start to feel the energy begins to slow down… Some relief starts in my body… But I know it is not totally over yet… I close my eyes and put my head back… Something else comes up and I write it down… Then again… Then again…

Until I Feel it is done… Total relief in my whole body… In my chest… Totally drained… Extremely hungry… Have to immediately get up and eat something… When everything is written I have the urge to eat as if there were no more food left in the world… Not really for the amount of food that I eat… But for the way that I eat it… And drink plenty of water… My breathing automatically becomes very deep... Very refreshing... Very fulfilling… A sense of total out this world happiness… A sense of joy… Total beauty…

As I explained before… It is very bothersome to try to resist against these energies… Extremely painful and difficult…

Even after having gone through them several times… And knowing exactly how the process goes for me… I start to resist them with all my being because I either do not have the time that I know it will take me… Or I am tired and do not want to spend the huge amount of energy that I know it will take … But… Like I said… It is such a potent kind of energy that totally sweeps me away and I end up having to surrender every time... Every single time... Even though I try to distract myself...

Many times I distract myself for days to helplessly have to end up sitting down to write... And write... And sense... And feel... And write... More... And more... And more... Until at some point the energies slow down... What had accumulated between my lower belly and my throat is emptied out from by body... And I know I am done... It is over... For now... Until the next surge of energy begins...

Many times I get a sensation similar to a headache... But is not really a headache... This sensation lasts sometimes hours or even days... And I know it is caused by the huge amount of heat that reaches my head...

Every time that these "energy cycles" happen to me… I get the sensation in my throat as if I had a sore throat… And again, I know it is because that huge amount of energy that circulates throughout my body during those times produces so much heat in me that it actually burns… And I get the evidence of this burning in a way of a sore throat… And on my lips…

My lips feel extremely hot during this process… And then at the end… When everything finishes and I look at myself in the mirror… They are actually burnt… Like when there is very cold weather and the lips burn sometimes… Or like when one spends the whole day at the beach in full sun… I can actually see it…

Every time this happens… While the energies are moving throughout my body… My eyes feel like two balls of fire… I can see the white part turn a little reddish… Again, because of the heat… They turn very shiny… Bright… Open… Beautiful… Almost like glowing… That is the sensation I feel…

The one thing that remains even after the energies "dissipate" is this beauty in my eyes… They have never turned back to the opaque, lifeless way they were all the previous years prior to when all this began… Never again… So noticeable that people look at me sometimes and ask me… "But what is it? … Something about you lately… Your eyes look different… Do you put lenses on them to change the color???" … And no… Nothing… All natural!!!! …

I know exactly what it is… But I have learned not to even start to try to explain any of this to anyone because they would not understand… I know it because I have tried many times… With the "simpler-to-understand" things that have happened to me during the last couple of years… And they tune me out after the first minute or two of my attempt to explain "whatever it is" that we are talking about…

I have understood… After so many attempts… That this is something that people will understand as they themselves are ready for it… Exactly as what happened to me throughout all this process… Just like this!!! … As if "by magic!!!!" …

During everything that goes on within me before I actually surrender and sit down to write… And many, many times even while I am writing… So much comes to me!!! … Much of it stays even if I do not write it until days later…

Other times I sit down to write and write and something comes… And the minute I try to remember what it is and write it down… It disappears from me… And there is no way I can get it back... That is (or used to be) extremely frustrating because I can still feel it inside of me... I can clearly sense it... But I cannot remember what it said...

After all this time I have learned to trust this... And if I cannot remember it after the first or second try, I just let it go... And move up to the next phrases and ideas that continue to steadily and intensely build up inside of me...

During the days prior to the time I feel the actual urge and rush... I know it is inevitable... Like a volcano that is about to erupt... There is a gradual build up of "things" in me... I usually have to stop many, and any, activities to write things down... Even driving... I have to pull to the side... Write things down on whatever piece of paper I can find... And then continue...

It is curious that throughout the years something made me not to throw those pieces of paper away... Even though I am the type of person that always throws everything away... Or ends up not finding things... But for some reason those little papers were always precious to me...

Then the resistance comes... Then the surrendering and the "giving up" ... And when I actually sit down and write... It is a combination of what was captured in all the pieces of paper (sometimes it is extremely hard for me to understand what I wrote, due to how fast I had to write it to be able to keep up with what was coming out)... Of what had accumulated inside my body... And what flows through me and from me at the moment of writing it... Not really from me... I am not sure where it all comes from... Let's just say "what flows at the moment" ...

One of the things that has tremendously amazed me from the very beginning is the fact that whatever flows, flows… And when everything stops, I do not have to edit much… Maybe just what I misspelled because of the intensity of the speed of writing… Or maybe some punctuation marks… Or capitalization… But what is written, is written… My fingers move without my mind knowing what is being written… And when I think I know where the writing is going… After I read it I realize it is something totally different…

And it delights me because… Even though the same happens every single time… It still amazes me how… After I read everything once… I have to end up reading it and reading it and reading it many times because it is as if it was not written by me…

And every time I read it again… I find some type of message… Something that goes very deeply inside of me and helps me to reflect… To understand… To Know something extremely meaningful to me…

Chapter 6-- The Way I Am **NOW**

Now... This is the very first time (end of April, 2015) that I feel exactly the same way about writing... Exactly the same energies... The same feelings... The same impulses... The same "filling up my body" by something greater that me... Something that does not originate in me... And since THAT BEING has spent quite some time without communicating with me... I can... For the first time... Isolate this marvelous process...

For the first time I go through this... And I know it was not caused by THIS BEING... But even now I cannot be totally sure that THIS BEING is out of this equation because even in these conditions... There is not a second in my life that THIS BEING is not with me... Under my skin... Behind my eyeballs... Inside of me... I have never had that feeling before... It is like I am constantly communicating with IT... I don't ever feel alone...

For a few months now I had the idea... The feeling... That I wanted to write... But could not get myself to do it... The build-up of ideas and sensations and feelings happens inside of me... But I cannot get myself to move a hand to at least write anything on pieces of paper... It is as if there is no purpose... Since THIS BEING is so distant from me...

Well... That is except the few times that it has happened with letters I have written to two amazing people I met in a trip I will describe a little later... Or with a couple of specific letters to very specific people... In very specific situations...

And I know these particular letters have not been created by me… They have also flowed "from somewhere else" instead… I know it because the process to write them was exactly the same as what I described before… And the way they were written is clearly not the way that the "ME" that has lived in my body all those first 42 years of my life writes…

But… This is the first time that it is just "me with me" … Without the expectation that someone close to me will read it… Without doing it for somebody else… Just for me… And now… For the past three days… I cannot stop writing… And it flows… And it flows… Like it isn't me…

I have come to a Knowing in this process… This time… I guess because I have not had the luxury of the distraction of THIS BEING's presence… I have been able to Feel and internalize something I explained to THIS BEING many times before… This "something" that happened when all this overwhelming energy… And temperature… And "everything-else-increase" happened inside of me every single time the build-up of writings to THIS BEING took place in my body…

This time I was able to experience… All "by myself" … What I felt and experienced and went through so many times in the process of writing to THIS BEING… Something that many times extended over several days… This time I was able to experience it deeper than ever…

This increase in energy… Sometimes very abrupt and without "previous notice" … Some other times trickling in almost unnoticed… Until by the time I realized it… There was nothing I could do to "stop it" … Other than go through it… And let mySelf flow with it… And be in total harmony with it… And love and understand myself and my body in the process… And write… And write… And write… And eat desperately when my energy was totally depleted due to the huge amount of energy "invading my body" very abruptly… And staying there… At a constant high… Over long periods of time…

And loving and understanding myself at the times I was totally paralyzed… Due to the exhaustion my body felt for all this intense energy and intense writing… To then experience another quick surge of ideas… Thoughts… Energies… Movement in my hands… Sensations in my body… And write… And write… And write… And write…

And the feeling in my chest… As if it was a balloon about to explode… And the feeling in my belly… Where I sense all this energy originates… And the feeling in my lower back… And on my head… And on my whole skin… And in my

Whole Being... And the overwhelmingly intense... But at the same time delightful movement of "something" throughout my whole body... From my belly to the "balloon" that developed in my chest... And from there to my head... And at times I even think at any moment there will be smoke coming out of my head :) ...

I could describe "that something" in many different ways that I have NEVER felt before... And the more I write... The more everything accelerates and intensifies inside of me...

So... The way I sense this whole process is that this increase in energy inside of me causes an increase in vibration in every particle inside my body... This is why it feels... As I have explained to THIS BEING many times... As if my body is like a balloon that is being inflated and inflated... The particles separating... And separating... And expanding... And expanding... The particles in my body vibrating faster and faster due to the increased energy… This increase in energy causes them to eventually separate a little more… And a little more… To the point that they can easily transition from solid to liquid to gas… And from there continue to separate more and more and more…

Until my skin becomes so thin due to this expansion… That it cannot hold anymore… But instead of just exploding like a balloon… My skin can easily disintegrate… Together with my whole being… And let that "energetically-gaseous" substance that is now my body mix with the surrounding air and energy and totally disappear by "dissolving" in it… By "becoming one" with it…

Could it be that this Knowing that came to me so clearly in this few days… Clearer that ever… Could it be that this is exactly what happens to my body when my whole being goes through this process???? ... I just have the sense to... At that critical point... Do something to slow down the energies a little... So I can stay in my body and stay in this world a little longer :) ... Everything is so beautiful!!!!

In many letters to THIS BEING before... I have explained sensations in similar way... But always thinking I was "making things up" ... Since I always felt those explanations were not truly coming from me...

And now... Same explanation... But very detailed... Very clear... Clearer than ever...

As I explained before... The very first times I went through this process of writing to THIS BEING... I was somewhat worried... But never had the impulse to go to the doctor and have myself checked...

Perhaps the fact that I always assumed THIS BEING was the reason I was feeling that way… Made me know that I was experiencing some type of Love that I had never experienced in my whole life…

A Love so divine… So miraculous… So pure… So beautiful and powerful and unstoppable… That I was convinced back then… And I am still pretty sure now… That I would never experience it again (but I do have doubts about this one)… And that at least 90% of people go through life and leave this world without ever experiencing THAT to the fullest extension… For one reason or another…

And despite all the "unbearable results" this process caused in my body every time… Somehow I sensed… Even in my most disoriented beginnings of going through "this" … That it was something good... Something unique that was happening to me... I just had the impulse NOT to act... Just let it flow through me... Just let myself flow with it... Just let my body live all this process...

And when everything was done... Every single time... The Joy... The sense of calmness... The Knowing that I am different afterwards... Many physical signs in the days and months to come that my body has experienced healing... In different ways every time... But always healing... One way or another... Always lighter... Always fulfilled... Always bathed and inundated with Love...

Chapter 7-- The "Theory" Of **GETTING OUT OF FOCUS**

During my child's "exercises" … As I was coming down the stairs from leaving my child in the second "class" … I was writing and reading about other things before then… And I climbed down the stairs in a desperate manner… Desperate to get to the laptop… And I write… And write… And I cannot stop writing…

Sometimes I feel that to be able to truly Feel and perceive… And to be in contact with my impulses… I have to get somewhat "out of focus" … It is as if I need my five senses not to be so involved in the situation… It is as if this way I would gain some type of "aerial view" …

But in reality is not "aerial view" ... It is a way of feeling and perceiving to which I have never been used to... And of which I had never realized up to this instant when I remembered the numbered items below... In that order... Like "lightning bolts" that came to my mind... And about the one that is not numbered I remembered as I type this paragraph...

I just realized that the essence of all those things is exactly the same... Getting out of focus... Getting out of the body a little to be able to perceive in a more "global" way... Or maybe it is not really "getting out of the body" ... It is more accurate to say that since the five senses are not so involved... As if they were roots or knots that tie themselves to what is directly in contact with them... Without letting us "see" beyond what is right in front of us...

As we detach a little from our five senses we can then have a little more access to "That" which is always with us… Our energy… Our guide… I don't know how to call it!!! … "That" which so many people… Including me up until a few years ago… Do not even consciously realize that exists… And that is always there… Ready… Available…

That term "getting out of focus" occurred to me one time… Without me knowing why… In one of those letters that write themselves in me for THAT BEING… I had never used that word in my life… And it was very curious to me that even though I was writing about other things… What was suddenly writing itself "on paper" was about the importance of "getting out of focus" …

And now… Many months after that… Without ever using that term again… And without even remembering about it ever again… That term comes suddenly to me... As something that downloads itself in me out of nowhere... And I have to write... And write... And write without break until that fluid stops... And the most beautiful thing about that fluid is not even what I write on the "paper" ...

The most beautiful is what I Feel in my body... In my eyes... In my chest that is about to explode... Many, many times I have to stop because it is such an intense kind of energy that runs throughout my body... So intense that in that peak moment I have to stop anything and everything I am doing... And just wait... And allow and Feel that energy flowing throughout my body...

And in that peak moment whatever was trying to write itself down is not written... Because it is impossible to even move a finger under those conditions... But I feel that what is happening inside my body is extremely important... More important than anything else... Even much more important than myself... It is like a type of blessing...

And I am very thankful to My Universe for this... And for having had patience with me all this time during which I was not understanding what was happening in me... For Loving me during all those moments in which perhaps doubt or fear used to dominate me... For having Loved me in all those prior moments of my life...

Especially in all those years in which I was the most disconnected from mySelf... And for always being there... Always... Until I finally reached that beautiful point in my existence... That point... So sublime and so marvelous and so pure... That point from which I am very convinced now there is no return... Absolutely no return...

1. The way I was able to realize that something that was almost about to happen… Should not happen… Something happened to us… The bank that we always used… To which we belonged ever since we moved to this city… Was unexpectedly closing its doors in the place that it had always been located… And was moving to the western extreme of the city… Very far… Extremely far from where we live…

And that… In this world in which we live… With such incredible technology… In which almost everything is done online… Should not be a problem for anyone… But for us it is a huge problem… For the specific conditions of our lives… For the lack of time… For how tight my schedule is… Because everything in our lives takes place in the eastern part of the city…

So having to suddenly go to the western part of the town… At least once a month… In the specific times that this bank works… It is just totally impossible…

But in the specific situation of me and my mom… It is better to stay there… Even under those new and very difficult conditions… Moving to a closer and more flexible bank would mean having to practically change our whole lives…

But the more we thought and thought about it… The more we analyzed my schedule and the bank schedule back and forth… And analyzed all the possibilities… And we realized that no way! … It is impossible to even think about going there if even just once a month…

And using the available technology for everything would not work for us…

So we decided that we had no other option… We had to find a bank that was closer to us and more flexible than the one we had… Even if that meant that we had to leave some formal things in that other bank… So… We asked around and finally decided to become members of a bank much closer to my mother's home…

We went there one day… And from the very beginning there was something I did not like very much… The employees… Because there were not many customers at the moment… Were all talking behind the counter… Laughing in a very loud manner… Somewhat similar to when one enters in a conversation when there are many people gathered in a backyard celebrating something and having a good time… They were like that during a couple of minutes… Without even taking a second to interrupt their conversation and see what we wanted…

Finally a very friendly gentleman approached us and asked us to go to his "office" …

He was so exaggeratedly friendly and so talkative that everything just went to the other extreme… And my mother was totally enchanted with all that friendliness and all that conversation…

We explained to him that we both needed to open accounts there… And we explained the reason why we needed to do it… Etc… So he decided… Maybe out of courtesy… To start with my mother… And I was very involved in all of that… Very actively… More or less during the first ten minutes…

But there was a point where my five senses could not take so much exaggerated "sweetness" anymore… And everything came to a point where it looks like they became somewhat disgusted with so much "sweetness" … So directly… That they had to disengage a little… Probably so they could continue to be able to assimilate all that conversation without getting to the very extreme of being totally disgusted...

The fact is that as the five senses were able to disengage a little from that conversation... My whole being went up to a different state... I cannot say that my Being reached an "ingravity" state per se... Because that is impossible as long as I am on this planet :) ... But my Being was truly able to reach a total "out of focus" state...

And in that moment I was able to be in that state of "aerial view" ... Without being totally "tied" to what was directly in front of me by my five senses... And that allowed me to start to see... Or not really to see... To feel very clearly what was happening... And to perceive in a very different way what that gentleman was telling us... And I could not be totally engaged anymore...

I had the need to start to look at my phone… As if I was reading something… With the excuse in my mind that he was dealing with something directly related to my mother, not me… So I had no reason to be directly involved in that…

And the moment came when he finished with my mom's account and started with mine… And when I gave him my personal information he went into an office… And we did not see him anymore in a long time… And he came back with the same frantic (unrestrained) gentleness… But explaining to me that… I am not sure due to what situation I had ten years ago… They could not "benefit" me in the same way as they did to my mother… (And they were already going to even charge her I do not know what amount for not having direct deposit) …

So what he was explaining to me… In all his excessive kindness… Was something like… They were doing a huge favor to me… They would allow me to open an account there and… I do not know what else he was going to say… I simply interrupted him and said… "But what do you mean? … That your supervisor is telling me that as a favor they are going to do that?" … And he was starting to explain that was correct… Very kindly… That for this reason and for this other reason… With all that "unleashed" kindness and friendliness…

To which I said "Oh no! … I thank you… But under those circumstances I am the one that does not want to open the account… I really do not want anyone to feel that this is a favor they are doing to me" … And it seems that there was some kind of powerful communication between us… A kind of communication that is much more powerful than words or even thoughts…

A communication that does not need any time to travel from transmitter to receiver… It happens at the same instant in the people directly involved…

He got this right away while it took my mom a few seconds to realize what was going on… And when she realized about it… She started to act in a very disoriented way… Trying to persuade me to change my mind…

But he did not do anything like that… Because at that split second when that instantaneous communication happened between us… His face… His whole Being instantly transformed… All that layer of excessive friendliness and kindness instantly washed away from him… And a very unpleasant and even rude expression took over his Whole Being…

We walked away from there and my mom was in a mix of feelings and thoughts… Between her amazement at how I was able to have such mental clarity and stand in such determination… And her worry about her account now opened there and I would not be there… And her concern about how rude I had been… Looking at my phone while he was talking…

And I started to explain to her… And she really did not understand what I was trying to explain… So I gave up trying and just told her not to worry about anything…

And yes… "Life" has a way to solve everything when we are open to it and allow ourselves to flow with it…

So now my mom's account in that bank is successfully closed… And we have found ways to happily continue to use our old bank… Ways that we could not even see or feel before… But that we were totally able to sense once we were fully able to realize that this is the direction in which we needed to go…

2. The way I was able to allow something that was senselessly stuck… To flow once and for all… My mom very astonished by something I told her… She suddenly said: "But I am very impressed by all that huge mental strength you have lately… What do you mean by *"Instead of senselessly pushing a wall, I prefer to let it dissolve by itself and then I go through without any effort"*? … That phrase is very interesting!" …

There was something very unbelievable that took place in my life… About a month ago… And everything happened in a very absurd manner… And even in a very adverse way… Around something so simple… The purchase of a small tablet… In the main store where they are sold and the connections for the Internet and phone services are made…

What 95% of people would have done… What I would have done in those first 42 years of my life… And what my mom had spent about a month insisting me to do… Insisting even to the point of getting upset with me many times… Is to go to the store to discuss this matter… Call this place or the other… Enter into that trouble and that never ending wear…

And I… Totally inert… Without knowing if I am doing the right thing or not… But my instinct is telling me to do absolutely nothing… Or maybe it is that I am not really feeling any signs from my instinct… And that does not allow me to take any kind of action… Not even be mad at my mother when she insists and pushes me a little too much…

And there I was... Totally inert about that topic... Seeing how the events unfold themselves... In total amazement about the absurdity of the situation... Seeing how one thing causes another one even more unbelievable... More absurd... But without being able to find the energy to do something about it...

Not out of frustration or fear or anything like that... It is simply as if... About that particular topic... I wasn't truly inside my body and everything was just happening through me... Without any of my five senses being able to involve themselves too much in any of that...

Something as if I did not have any desire to spend my energy in any of that... Immovable...

My monthly plan expired yesterday... And I tried... And there was no way I could be able to enter my information and put more money into the account…

Without any kind of information about the tablet to be able to call… My mother… When I told her: "But I am going to call and what am I going to be able to tell them? … That I am calling to add money to a tablet but I do not even know which one it is… Or what is the number assigned to it… Or anything… What do you think they will say?" … "But how can we solve anything in this way, dear customer?" … "Nooo… I just cannot call! … Without at least knowing what is the phone number that identifies the tablet" … And my mom started to have one of those "nervous laughter attacks" … And she could not stop laughing…

I tried to enter two days ago in their Internet site… Entered my information… And nothing! … At the end of every attempt they kept telling me that they could not find me... And I had not been able to find where I put the number of the tablet... To see if they would be able to find me that way...

Suddenly that afternoon something similar to a text came in... They were telling me that I had not paid the monthly amount... And that text disappeared in an instant...

And I was not able to find it again since it wasn't sent through the "normal" way... And there I was... In total desperation... "My God!!! ... But how did I allow this text to disappear like that? ... Maybe it contained some type of information that could help me!!!!!" ...

And whatever was in that text escaped from me "as water through my fingers" ... But that was the first sign that at least something was moving around this topic... It was not stagnant anymore...

Nothing to do at that precise moment though… So I went on with my life…

The next day… Very early in the morning… I opened the tablet to at least charge it a little bit… I suddenly see a text… Similar to the previous one… I put myself in total attention so it would not disappear from me… In that moment I was in a hurry because I had to take my mother to doctors' appointments… I made sure to close the tablet very carefully so when I open it again the text will be there…

I came back from all the errands I had to run and… How happy I was to see that this marvelous text was there waiting for me!!! … And in the most calmed way I allowed my instinct to guide me in each step I should take… And from one step I started to discover the next… And following that path I was able to find the number of the tablet… And was able to enter my information in their

Internet site... And was able to add the monthly amount of money to the account...

And just like that... As I suddenly and in a very calmed manner told my mother that day... After a month of going through this sequence of unbelievable absurds and total desperation: *"Instead of senselessly pushing a wall, I prefer to let it dissolve by itself and then I go through without any effort"* ... And five months of me happily using the tablet have passed by already... In total flow... In total Joy :) ...

3. The way I have been able to feel... Truly Feel... THAT BEING... So intensely... So uniquely... As I was thinking about what I wrote in the previous paragraphs I remembered many things I feel with THAT BEING... And ITS insistence to involve the five senses as much as possible... And my "almost necessity" of involving the senses the least possible the majority of the times… And perhaps that has been what has allowed me to Feel THIS BEING in such a way in which I have not been able to feel anyone… Even when they may have shared my same space and all my five senses… Could this be part of the reason why everything has happened in the way that it has happened in respect to THIS BEING????? …

*** The way I have been able to flow… Truly flow… In my "dance" classes… And in all my other exercise classes…** For a little less than two years I have been attending a gym… And even though I take several classes there… There is a particular one that I have come to love very deeply…

And like in many other things that have happened to me in the past two years… If someone would have ever told me that I would be going to a gym… And especially doing "that" type of class…

I would have thought that person was totally crazy…

Not for anything in particular about the gym or the class… But because of the way my personality has been all those first 42 years of my life… I have always been very shy... And I have always been very… Well… I have described all that enough and do not think I have the desire to go back to even think about that ever again… At least not more than absolutely necessary…

Anyways… I still remember that day when I went there for the first time… The class was full… And the majority of the people in the class were 65 years old and beyond… And even though in my younger years I always liked to dance… And I did it pretty well… When I got to the class… I was lost!!! …

And not only was I lost… My body could not resist… Even though I had been walking and doing exercise on my own for the previous ten months…

And all those people that I would not have expected to be able to do any of those moves and steps started to look at me and started to encourage me and even taught me many tricks to be able to learn faster… They became a true source of inspiration and the main reason why I did not give up on it at those early beginnings…

I went from one instructor to the next on the different days of the week… And as the first couple of months went by… I was, slowly but surely, getting more comfortable with the whole process… But I still felt that even though I was getting pretty good at it… There was something missing…

And I couldn't really tell what was missing… I was being able to pretty much dance just like the teachers… Except, of course, anything involving bending my knees… But that is part of another story :) … Like I said… I could not pinpoint exactly what was missing even though I could clearly sense it…

And the instantaneous clarity came a few days after a different instructor started to take over most of the classes at the time of day that I could attend the gym… The types of movements and the parts of the body that needed to move and the variety of the dances and the steps were simply impressive…

One had to really pay attention to be able to follow… So I started to try not to miss even a second of what the instructor was doing… I guess I was doing that out of the obsession of being a perfectionist… But I felt stiff and constricted…

Something was not quite right… And again… I could sense it but I could not pinpoint exactly what it was…

Until one "magical day" when I realized that "that day" … And a few days prior to "that one" … I was flowing… Truly flowing… Flowing to the point that I didn't really know what I was doing… Flowing to the point that I did not remember what was happening…

And I thought "I better pay attention, or I am going to be lost!" … And the minute I started to truly pay attention and trying to count every step the teacher was doing… And to copy every movement… And so forth and so on… I instantly felt that my body was not flowing as much… That I became somewhat stiff and constricted again…

And my movements and steps were being as perfect as the teacher's… But I was not feeling that Inner Flow… That Magical Flow that brings beauty to everything we do…

And I was very intrigued by this… And I started to think about the few days prior to that… Those days that I had felt those "flashes of magical flowing" … I had felt them, but I had not realized at the moment… And… Again… When I started to use my five senses a little too much… Either some step went wrong… Or I missed a turn… Or I paid too much attention… Most of the times in a critical way… To how my body was moving… I was just not flowing as in those few times when I had Lived and Felt those "flashes of magical flowing" …

And I remember everything coming to a point when I said… Or thought to mySelf… "You know what? … Who cares? … I am just going to disconnect myself and just flow with it… " … And one day… Several days after that… I had a very deep experience…

I realized I was truly flowing… Totally flowing… To the point that I realized that my body was there… Performing all the dances… All the steps… Going through all the motions… But the True Me wasn't so much there… It was as if the True Me was floating somewhere close to the ceiling… Or up in the clouds… So beautiful!!! …

And I experienced something I had experienced so many times before… For so many years already!!! … I was meditating!!! …

My body was there dancing… But The True Me was meditating… Without me having even the slightest intention to do that… It was such a delightful experience!

Now I became really excited because… Honestly… For the last few months I had tried to meditate… But could not get mySelf to do it… I wanted to do it… I Loved the feeling of it… But did not have the patience… So much eagerness in me… So much energy all the time… So much that I nearly always felt the True Me was like a playful ball bouncing off my body all the time… Not wanting to be still… Not wanting to be restricted… Not even wanting or needing to sleep many times… So happy!!! … So Joyful!!!

But I loved the sensations and the feeling that meditating always brought to me… So… Maybe without me consciously knowing… I started to… In my mind… See and reflect on how I was able to do that… And I realized that my eyes were usually staring at a metal object that stuck out of the ceiling… Like a water outlet for the fire extinguishing system or something like that… Other times my eyes were staring at the mirror… But not at me… Or at any particular person or object… Just in a type of "unfocused gaze" in the direction of the mirror… And the moments I needed to look at something… I would look at the instructor's feet… To sense the steps she was doing… To then quickly "get lost" in the cuddling arms of myTrueSelf again…

Now my eagerness to go to that class was multiplied at least by a hundred… Not only was I exercising my body and feeling great! … But I was also able to Feel that Magical Flow with all my intention and with all my Being… And I was being able to meditate again :) …

Yes… It is a different type of meditation… Perhaps most people would not call that "meditation" … But it works wonders for me… And it makes me feel total Joy and Love… And appreciation of my world… And of Me…

And then I realized that the other classes that I also loved so much… And knew were so beneficial for my body… Were staying behind in my "priorities"… And something inside of me did not want that to happen… So I started to "unintentionally" sense ways to incorporate those "meditation-like" feelings into them…

And I would have thought that is nearly impossible… Since those other classes involve different sizes of dumbbells… And bars… And exercise balls… But the inner "unintentional" drive… Or desire… That I had to do it appears to have been much more powerful than all the doubts in the world put together…

So I started with the most "automatic" and "steady" routines… And it was so fulfilling to me to feel that Wholeness that I felt for the first time ever… And I have been more and more "submerged" in this experience and in this feeling… To the point that I am now able to do the majority of the routines of that one-hour class with my eyes closed… Being one with mySelf…

And I am joyfully watching me going back to a couple of classes I had stopped attending… And I am enjoying them like I never did before… In total communion with mySelf… Just me with Me… Regardless of how many other people are in the room at any particular moment…

****

And writing about all of this I realize that it is not to change the attention and to focus on something else… It is to continue with the attention and the Intention on "that" … Whatever "that" may be… But without having our five senses 100 % involved with it… So this way we are able to attach ourselves a little less to "that" and merge a little more with "That" that we always have around us… Inside of us… "That" which allows us to Feel and perceive in a way that is much more extensive… More intense…

Complete… Clear… Lucid… Full… And… Yes… In the precise cases… Pleasurable…

Chapter 8 -- If This Isn't ABUNDANCE...
Then What Is It?

I was already used to be flowing "very high" for the last few months... Living in pure magic... With all the events... Big... Small... Medium... Events of all kinds and magnitudes presenting themselves in my daily existence at the precise moment... In the precise amount... In the precise fashion...

Without me even asking for absolutely anything... As I used to do in my "previous life" ... In which I "hung on" to things I believed I wanted... And asked with deep intensity every night at bedtime... Or I used to light candles with specific wishes and things along those lines...

Now that I realize it... Since the last couple of years I do not do any of that...

It was nothing pre-planned... It has been something completely gradual... Completely imperceptible... I have realized about it just now... As I write this...

But yes... These last few months everything has come practically to a point in which I think of something and it is suddenly there... As the most natural thing in the world... And when I see it or feel it... I realize "that" was exactly what I was thinking about or desiring in that precise moment... Everything in a very subtle and "natural" way...

It is so interesting to me how everything is coming to be... So much "unbelievable" abundance in my life but... Again... It is not unbelievable to me anymore... It is becoming the most normal thing in my world... And something that amuses and excites me... But does not surprise or amaze me like it did before... It does keep an eternal smile on my face... An infinite joy in my eyes... An intense happiness in my being...

And even though I could go on forever with stories and memories of the endless details of synchronicities and abundance in my daily life during these past couple of years... There are two of them that have a very special place in my heart for the overwhelming attention to details that Life... Or the Universe... Or... Or... Or... (the name does not really matter) ... Put together to make me realize the magnitude of what was taking place at that moment of my life...

---The Trip to the Seaquarium---

One day of April of 2015... At 10:56 a.m. ... My child's teacher sends an email that talks about this trip for the first time... Asking if parents were approving of their child going... 9 minutes later I replied to her and said "Absolutely!" ... She did not answer anything else until about a week later... And I responded how happy I was about their trip and how much we LOVE that place...

I talked to my mom about me telling the teacher that if they needed parents to volunteer, I would be delighted to go... And my mom was very excited for me to go... And she thought it was a great idea for me to volunteer... Because that way I could be close to my child... Since they would be so far from home...

And I just kept thinking... In very deep excitement... How much fun it would be for me to spend this day with my dear child, classmates, and teachers... In this environment that we've come to love so much since two years ago... And what an incredible experience it would be for my child to see me there... Since this young mind only associates that place with family... Not with something school-related... And to combine everything in one place... So far from home... Will be quite unique for this little mind... And very delightful to me...

In the meantime... My child's teacher sent out a general email saying that since there has been such interest among parents to volunteer to this event... She will find out the amount of money that parents would need to pay for the entrance tickets... And that the children's tickets were covered by the school... But parents willing to go would have to pay for their tickets... And in my mind I said "Great!!! ... Things are moving along!" ...

Then one Monday... Already in May... As I was sitting at the bench during my child's Soccer session... Somewhere around 6:30 p.m. ... One parent from my child's class asked me if I was going to the Seaquarium with the kids... And my eyes illuminated as I said "Yes!!!! ... I LOVE that place!" ... And he goes on talking about how he doesn't know how much the ticket is... And that it is probably too expensive... And that he did not know whether we all fit in the bus...

And I said that I wanted to go anyways... Talked about the different shows and how they compare to the ones in the more famous Seaquarium in another city... And I told him about the day we sat right on the spot where the whale lifts that impressive wall of water... And what an experience that was! ... And how we had never expected it to be something SO powerful... And what happened to my dad's camera as a result of it... And how my child was scared and somewhat paralyzed at first... And then quickly got over it... And was even amused by the experience... And on... And on...

And then I explained to him that I was sure we would be asked to drive our cars... Since all the school buses are so small and barely have enough room for the students and their teachers… And that I would want my child to go in the bus… To have the full "classroom" experience learning about the ocean habitat… And I would just follow the bus… And maybe on the way back bring my child with me… And depending on the time, we would stop by grandpa's house and spend a few minutes with him… Or if not… If other parents wanted to carpool… I would just carpool with them… And perhaps bring the kids on the way back with us… Or just follow the bus again…

None of it mattered to me at all… Inside of me the only thing that was present was eagerness… Anticipation… Fun… All kinds of nice expectations about how much we would enjoy that day… I looked up the prices and told him… And he still was not convinced… And I kept saying that I was going anyways… And how happy I was about going… Still expecting my child's teacher's follow-up email with the directions for what parents needed to do, the prices, etc...

And... The next day... Not even 24 hours later... I received an email from her... Directed to me and two other parents... Saying that we were the first three parents that expressed interest in going with the kids... And since there was some money left over... Our entrance to the park was covered...

Honestly... I was not expecting that at all... I was just waiting for the follow-up email with the instructions... And was extremely happy about being able to go and have that experience with my child... But at the same time all I said was "Thank you, Universe!!!" ... And felt it as the most natural thing, and something really normal... I, of course, did not expect these specific details... I was just expecting everything to be GOOD... And it turned out to be more delightful and amusing than anything I had ever imagined...

Some days passed by without major thinking about the trip on my part... Well... That is not really true... I had been so excited about it... Soooo excited!!! ... I told all my close people about it... The ones close by... And the ones far away... In my mind I am constantly thinking about it... And I do not even know why... We have been there already... I am not a kid anymore...

That is part of my comment to everyone I talk to about it... The fact that I am not a kid anymore and I am more excited than if I were one... My mom gave me a blue "Life Is Good" T-shirt... And I automatically said "I am going to wear this one on the Seaquarium field trip" ... Then I said "I will wear it with my blue sunglasses" ... And then we went to the store for my mom to get some Mother's Day presents... And all I had in my mind was the field trip... So I ended up getting a blue backpack to be able to carry my child's food easier… And at the same time wear something that matches with the Seaquarium… And blue shoes…

I kept telling the story of how lucky I was to my closest people… Amused by how things were happening… Without me even thinking that any of that was possible…

Last night at soccer practice another parent asked me whether I was going to the field trip… And I said "Of course!" … Then whether I was driving my car… And whether I was meeting them at school… And whether I was taking my child in the car with me or in the bus with the teachers and the kids…

To which I said that yes… I was driving my car… And I was going to meet them early at school… Which I thought was what everybody would do… And that for the trip to the Seaquarium

I prefer that my child rides with teachers and classmates in the bus… And I follow in my car… For the full experience of going on the field trip with everybody else… Otherwise… It would be like riding in the car with me… Just like going to any of the many places we go together… Just the two of us… And then I added that maybe if it was too late, I would take my child in the car with me on the way back… And that I did not mind if another parent wanted to ride with me… Etc… Etc…

The morning of the trip my child was tired because of a long day the day before… Bowling… Then soccer… And getting to bed later than I wanted to… And I miscalculated the time that morning… And got out of the house later than we needed to…

And one of my eyes was a little reddish because something had fallen in it… And I was thinking "What if they think I have a pink eye and

I will be contagious to the kids? ... I should stay and have them take my child" ...

And then I was thinking "But wait! ... I have been wanting to go on this trip for the longest time... For my child to have the experience... Etc... Etc... And I know I do not have a pink eye! ... I mean... It is pink... But not for the reason that people usually fear pink eyes" ... So I was with all that tug-a-war inside of me... To go? ... Not to go? ... Total indecision... Not a nice feeling at all... NO... That was a "normal" state of being for me before but... That's not who I am now! ... And then I said "I AM going!" ...

Got out of the house... And into the car... And realized "OhMyGood!!! ... I ended up not putting gasoline in my car last night... Well... I will rush to school because it is already late... Then I will have them take my child in the bus with them... I will follow them and if I make it to the place... Fine... And on the way back stop for gas... And if I see the gas is getting empty... Then I will stop for gasoline and catch up with them later"... So very short time to get to school!... But pretty good ride... We would have enough time to barely make it...

And all of a sudden... Almost right at the exit we needed to take for school... The traffic totally stopped... There were so many cars that it appeared there was no hope to at least start moving any time soon... I called the teacher and told her "We are almost at the exit... But the traffic stopped... Just leave and I will head south with my child and meet you there"... And she quickly goes "No... We will wait for you until you get here"... To which I did not have anything to respond... In my heart I was so appreciative of her words!... I just said "thank you" and hung up... Just in case other parents were also calling her...

At the second I hung up... The traffic cleared as if by magic... And it was such a smooth ride that we made it by the time they said they wanted to leave…

Getting to school parking lot was somewhat shocking to me… I was expecting to see at least five or six parents there… And the teachers already getting all the students in the vans… But… Nothing… Deserted…

Since it was much earlier than the start of the school day… The parking lot was deserted… I was lucky enough that the school bookkeeper arrived at that moment… I asked her and she thought they would have left by now… But said she would check for me anyways… Then one of the assistants came out… And I asked whether everybody was here already and she said no… And told me to bring my child inside and that I should come in too… I left everything in the car… Since I was going to follow them…

When I got in I showed the teacher my eye… And I explained I think it was in that condition because something had fallen in it… She said not to worry… I insisted… "But do you know why I am showing it to you???? … If you want I can just stay… I do not want anyone to feel uncomfortable thinking it is something else" … And she said "No… You stay close to us and do not worry about it!!!" … Then we got inside the classroom and there were three other students besides my child… Plus the teacher and the assistants… And no parents… And no other kids… One of the assistants gave me half of her coffee… Everybody was extremely happy and nice…

And then the teacher announced it is time to go!!! … So we started walking to the parking lot… And as we got out and I was going to head to my car… She goes… "You come in the red van with us" … And I said "Are you sure????? … I was thinking I will just follow you" … And she said "No… Just come with us… Two of the students that were coming are not here today… So we have extra room" … And I said "Oh, Thank you!!!!" … Ran out to my car to get my backpack and my child's lunchbox…

And I ended up going with them… Sitting in the front seat… Not having to drive my car all by myself… Not having to pay for the entrance ticket… Not having to worry about the empty tank… Not having to even pay for the gas for this trip!

It was a very pleasant trip… Getting to know my child's teachers on a more personal level… Talking about various topics… Even being silly at times… The kids were extremely well behaved… We got there and the seaquarium parking lot was totally empty… Only some of the parents and their kids were there… And the other ones arrived shortly after that…

It ended up being that apparently they decided to just go straight to the park and take their kids with them… I guess they did that to save time… I am not sure… But to me… It was more important for my child to have the full experience of the field trip… Even if it was going to mean a "waste of time and gasoline" … Since we live south… And the school is 20 minutes north of our house… And the park is about one hour and a half south of our house…

But spending all that extra time and extra driving was never even an issue in my mind… All that mattered to me was the fullest experience possible for my child :) … For the first couple of hours the park was almost completely "just for us"… It started to get full when we were about to leave… So it truly was an "out of this world" delightful experience…

They had announced rain for that day… So I was thinking about it for a few days… And thinking... "No!!! ... It is not possible that something so beautiful and so expected is going to get spoiled by the rain!" ... So I was kind of trusting that it was going to be just fine... And early that morning... Around 3:00 or 4:00 a.m. ... Very heavy rain... And I remember me thinking "Oh no! ... This is not possible! ... The kids are supposed to have a beautiful day!" ... Then I kept there... Laying on my bed... And around 6:00 a.m. ... The heaviest sudden rain I have ever seen... And I was like "What!?!?!?" ...

And then I remembered that for the past week... Whenever we would get on the highway in the morning to go to school and there was heavy... Almost not-moving traffic... I would tell my child "Let's see how we can ease out this traffic!!!!" ... And it had worked every time... All of a sudden... Every single time... It was as if that heavy traffic had never even been there... And we got to school in record time... Without any worries... Without any stress… Every time… And every time on my way back home I would still see the miles and miles of stuck, totally-not-moving-traffic still there… But we were miraculously out of it…

So… I remembered that… And said in loud voice "Let's ease out this weather!!!!!!" … Now I do not remember if I said it out loud… Or if I said it very loudly in my mind's voice… But I know I said it with all my Being… And all I know is that it was the most beautiful… Sunny day… Sunny… But breezy… Perfect for a place like that!!!! … All the kids were perfect… All of them were very happy… All the parents were happy… The teachers were very pleased…

We got back to school in perfect timing… Almost at the end of dismissal… The other parents with their kids went straight home from the park… My child and I went back to school with the classmates and teachers…

And had time to go home… Have a snack… Relax a little… And go to a 6:00 to 7:00 p.m. "exercise" class… And even though I thought the exhaustion would act against performance and behavior… It ended up being perfect… We got back home… Ate… Took a shower… Played a little… And then without many issues… My child cleaned up… Went to bed… And fell asleep…

Today my child has been full of energy the whole day… And… Something totally unexpected by me, by the way… Has been following along and doing an excellent job everywhere… So… Without me expecting any of this… Well… The only thing I was expecting and hoping was that they would let me go with them to the Seaquarium trip… Just let me go with them…

But then all these "miracles" … One after another… Totally unexpected… Totally "unimagined" … Started to happen… Out of nowhere…

And even the idea and the possibility of this trip came out of nowhere… I found out later that it was not something planned… It originated in my child's teacher's mind because of an unexpected gift the class received from somebody… And since they were learning about marine habitats… It was the perfect place to go…

And I ended up having a blissful experience… With well behaved happy kids… It was totally awesome… THANK YOU!!!!!!!!!

--The Trip to A 3.5-hr-Away-Country by Airplane--

Every time my child and I go to this very-loved-place… 2.5 hrs away from us by car… We can see the only elevations that exist in our entire area… I am sure my child could notice the landscape a little different… But did not know how to express it…

Just within this past year my child's vocabulary has started to build up a little… And around two months before the end of last school year… They learned the word "mountain" at school…

So… Our next trip to that very-loved-place was particularly special to me for two reasons… 1) When we passed by one of those garbage hills my child suddenly said "mountain" … And this was the very first time I heard my child use that word… Plus it was one of the first times my child had been able to use a word learned in school in "real life" … 2) In that moment I realized we needed to go to the "real place" … We needed to go to where my child could feel what a mountain is… And sense the special energy one feels when being immersed in such beauty…

I think this very special moment was the reason… The fuel… That made me start thinking in action terms.

Honestly… All my life… Since I moved to this area… I have been missing the mountains… And especially the first two years after all this started to happen to me… It has been a great need for me to see the mountains again… To feel them…

So… I guess I could not tolerate the fact that my child was misusing such special term to refer to the landfill hills… Every time we drove by those hills after that I would say: "This is not a mountain, Child-Of-Mine! … One day I will take you to see real mountains… I promise!!!" …

At that point… I had no idea how we would be able to do it… Where to go… And especially I could never imagine we would be traveling so soon…

I have always stressed out a lot about taking my child to places… Not so much anymore… I have to admit… But before it was always hugely stressful to me… Even to go to a store or a restaurant nearby…

The way my child's body did not respond properly the first years of life… Then my child started to grow and the behaviors and body movements were not the same as those of someone the same age… The way that many things would trigger spontaneous and many times disruptive behaviors… Especially when around people… Or in enclosed places… In stores… When standing in line… When the music was loud… Etc… Etc…

Then the fact that after I realized what was going on with my child… I decided to follow the path of a very strict... Natural diet... Where everything is made at home... Combined with the fact that my child is very selective in terms of food...

All of this causes us going places to be something much more than an adventure...

At the same time... I have always been of the opinion that we better "endure" things sooner than later... And that we need to be able to live a normal life... And the more exposed my child is to things and experiences... The more and the faster learning will take place...

And when I started taking my child places as early as 1 year old... I started to notice that somehow there was a tremendous expansion in awareness every time... My child's ability to incorporate new skills would increase... And so forth and so on...

And I always thought that we needed to do it "now"… Because later when my child became an adult… It would probably be too late to begin…

Anyways… We have never stayed home because my child would act one way or another… But I always made sure that either my father and his wife… Or my brother… Would go with us… I was worried that if something happened to me… Or if whatever unforeseen event took place… Etc… I would need somebody else to make sure my child would be fine… Plus with all the special diets… Etc… Being by myself would not be enough to carry everything… Plus make sure I could control the spontaneous behaviors… Etc… And always the fact that other people sometimes do not understand and may get upset stresses me a big deal…

One day… "Out of the blue" … I truly do not know out of where… Because this would have never occurred to me in my "sane" mind… But anyways… That day… Out of the blue… The idea of being in an airplane with my child and going through all that experience "was placed" in my mind… But where??? … How??? …

I guess my child's sudden "interest" in the mountains made me think it would have to be a place where we could see them… But at the same time I wanted it to be a very short trip… Non-stop… Since I was nervous about many things… Bathroom… Handling things… Finding places… My child's behavior… The other people… Etc…

The fact that a couple of months before I had reconnected with my school friend, who lives in that "3.5-hr-Away-Country-By-Airplane" … And that she insisted that we go visit… And that she will drive us… And take vacation… And cook for us... Etc... Made me decide to go... Since it would just be the airport/airplane experience... And a 3.5-hr flight... So... We would be taken care of here... Since my brother and my mom would be with us till the last minute at the airport... And my friend would be greeting us there and be with us the whole time till our return...

Despite all of that... I was still very undecided... Nervous... And stressed about it... But all that changed the minute the first "beautiful Angel" appeared in our lives...

Once the intention was in place... And the real hope to do it "germinated" within me... It was literally as if something in the Universe was switched to the "on" position... Which then made a very complex... But at the same time extremely simple mechanism of many different pieces... Big and small... That perfectly fit and worked together… To begin a beautiful motion process toward the completion of a dream…

First… My friend reappearing after about eighteen years… And using all her kindness and willpower to pull us out of our comfort zone and make me start thinking about this dream in very real terms…

Then… It was my child's teacher at school… Not the same I talk about in the Seaquarium experience… Another one… My child's teacher for the prior two years… A true Angel in our lives… An incredible Human Being who was always willing to help me in every possible way… So I could have better tools to be able to help my child…

I always felt very comfortable in talking with her about anything related to my child… And the minute I told her about the idea of going on an airplane... And how I wanted to give my child this experience... And at the same time how even the simple thought of it caused me to stress out so much...

In that instant this teacher... Without the slightest hesitation... Suggested that we should visit someone... And the teacher said she was sure this person would be more than willing to help us... And not only that... She even took the time to contact this person first... So then it would be easier for me (an extremely shy person), to get in contact with her and see how she could help us...

And in this simple way... Another True Angel appeared in our lives... Just like that... And from the first minute I spoke to her on the phone... I could sense this was a very special person... But I was never able to even imagine how truly special this person was... And all the beautiful and miraculous things that would unfold for us in the months prior to… And during our trip until we came back…

From that point forward… What I do not have any other way to describe… But as "an invasion of Angels" … Started to appear in our lives…

Many friends and family members that helped us in the most amazing ways… From "showering" us with monetary gifts that completely covered the expenses of our trip… To taking us to and picking us from the airport… To offering lots of advice about packing things and "tricks" to make the airport experience much easier for me and my child… To giving us many things we would need in our trip…

From someone not too close to me sending me a huge bag full of very comfortable and nice clothes that fitted me perfectly… To a mortgage company sending me a check... Out of the blue... For something related to a house that I used to own ten years ago...

From me thinking it would be nice if I could find one of those small travel bags... Where you put all the personal care items and when you get to the place, you just open the zipper and it has a hanger and it looks like a little cabinet where you keep everything at your fingertips... In a very nice way... I had seen an old one my dad has... But was never interested since we don't travel far... So the idea came to me and I had been looking for it in every store we went to... But had not been able to find one...

So I completely forgot about it... And one day as I was helping my cousin pack, since she was moving to another house... There was a pile of items that she no longer needed... And she told me to take whatever I would like... And as I looked at the items… There it was! … A brand new one… Still in its original package… Exactly as the one I was looking for… And my cousin had no idea I wanted one of those…

To many family members and friends offering to take care of our two dogs while we are gone… And the main thing that everyone showered us with was Love… Lots and lots of Love!!! …

Chapter 9-- ABUNDANCE... A Bottomless Pit Of **BLESSINGS** And **MIRACLES**...

---Our Two Senior Dogs---

Yes... From everything mentioned before... To even an "almost stranger" that helped us to take care of the last "problem" that could prevent us from actually going on the trip...

I... Kind of "by accident" ... Mentioned to her about the dream of our trip and how everything was coming along...

But the only thing that was stopping us now was the care of our two senior dogs... The trip would take eleven days and I did not feel comfortable about bothering anyone with this because I knew how busy everyone was…

At the same time I did not want to put our dogs in one of those "pet hotels" … I had tried that once before… Just for a couple of days… And was completely sure I did not want to put our dogs through that experience ever again… Plus… Since they were already old… They had many "issues" that would make me totally unable to allow somebody to keep them at their house…

But with this "almost stranger" it was totally different… That "coincidence" of the two of us being on the same sidewalk at the same time… Of the conversation to flow so seamlessly… Of how happy this lady was… Of how interested she was in us to be able to fulfill our dream…

So… When the conversation got to the point of me starting to mention about the dogs… Just for the sake of it… Because that was about the only thing that had been in my mind lately… This lady… This "almost stranger" just said "bring them to my house" …

To which I reacted by being instantly paralyzed… Almost not believing what I was hearing…

And I say "almost" because things were a little different this time… I was too far along in the process of "dealing" with this "invasion of Angels" as to not to realize that perhaps (most likely) this was another piece to complete "the whole" …

So… I went on with the conversation… Honestly… Knowing how I know me… I can tell you that in a previous stage of my life that conversation would not have even taken place… But I was able to recognize the probability of that being "another Angel" meant (or "sent") to help us to complete this dream…

At the moment this conversation took place… I wasn't even looking for anything… I was happily walking around my mom's neighborhood… Enjoying the air… Enjoying the clouds… Enjoying the beautiful day… And the whole sequence appeared in front of me as if "by magic" … "Out of nowhere" … And the sequence of words back and forth… And the "very fluid" flow of the conversation…

So even though I said that "No way! … I cannot bother her with this! … I cannot do that!" … And explained how old our dogs were… And the things that she would need to go through… This "almost stranger" insisted and said … "Why don't you bring them one day to visit and see how do they get along with my dog inside my house?" …

And there was no way that I could continue to offer resistance to the kindness of this "almost stranger"… To the kindness of this "Beautiful Being"…

So the day came when I took the dogs to her house… And what I saw was totally amazing… Her place was as if the house belonged to the dog and the human was just a visitor there… So many toys!… So many dog beds!… Everything was arranged around the needs and the likes of the dog!…

And the three dogs got along together very well… And this "almost stranger" did not seem to mind any of the arguments that I explained to try to convince her about how hard it would be for her to keep the three dogs…

All I could get from this "almost stranger" was always a smile... Always a welcoming attitude... And even refused to charge me anything to keep the dogs there... Absolutely nothing...

---The "Angel" Introduced To Us By My Child's Teacher---

This person is extremely busy... And after our first contact, she took the time to communicate with me... Both via emails and phone calls... To see what would be the most ideal way she could help my child... She took great care in finding out the details of our trip, so whatever she could do on her end would be the most beneficial to my child...

And we started communicating back in April... And the trip would take place in June and would last 11 days... And school was out at the beginning of May... So she suggested that in order not to disrupt my child's school life so much...

And in order not to do this too close to our departure, which would end up being more stressful than helpful for me… And in order to do this as close to our trip as possible, so everything was fresher in my child's mind… She suggested that we do it toward the end of May…

I asked about how long we should plan for our visit to be… Just to coordinate the rest of our activities that day… And I thought she would say fifteen to thirty minutes… And I was very surprised when she suggested that we planned for about two hours…

And I was delighted about her ability to put herself in both of our shoes… And analyze every little detail… And offer a very meaningful idea… But I was even more delighted at her willingness to spend so much time thinking about us and trying to plan the best possible experience for my child…

So the day we agreed on came… And I was expecting a quick tour through some of the waiting areas of the airport… I was expecting her to maybe show my child some aspects of going up to the ticket counter… Etc…

But how far I was from what we were going to experience!!! … The attention to details was impressive… The thoughtfulness was just unbelievable… The attention we received from so many people there that day was just totally overwhelming… Everything we got to see… To experience… So much Love from everyone! … So many smiles! … So many nice people! … So much advice and so many suggestions to me to make our experience easier… So much Love and care to my child…

And when we went in her office… She even had pictures on the wall of my child and his classmates when they went there on a field trip the previous year… I felt I was just floating on top of a cloud or something…

I am not going to talk about the specific and amazing details of these magnificent and unforgettable two hours because it would be just too much to mention… And… Honestly… I prefer to keep that in a very special place inside my heart… In that very special place where I keep my most precious treasures :) …

And we talked so much that day… She got to know part of my truest feelings about my child and our experience in this Life together… And at some point she said that yes… She was doing all of that for my child… But she was doing it even more for me… Because she wanted me to ease most of my stress… And because she could tell from the very beginning that I was an incredible human being… And because I was raising a wonderful child :) … Just for that :) …

That day all my emotions were at the very surface of my skin... Tears of Joy sometimes... And other times tears of truly not believing how these wonderful people could be so extremely nice to us... And so thoughtful... And so Loving...

And we left that place feeling so excited... Feeling so fulfilled... My child was feeling the owner of that place... Was definitely the owner of all of those hearts and Souls during the time he was there :) ... And if that would have been all that these wonderful people did for us... And if that would have been all that this Beautiful Angel did for us... It would have been way more than anyone would have ever expected... Much more than anyone would be able to dream about...

But NOOOO!!!! ... That was not all!!!! ... Many emails would follow... One saying that she had contacted the manager of the airport from which we needed to depart and that she was assured that we would be taken care of there… Another one saying that she contacted the manager of the airline in which we were flying and that they would make sure we would have the most pleasant experience…

And how totally unbelievable everything was to me is completely beyond description… And the only thing I could do in the midst of all my awe and all my amazement was to just say yes to everything that was coming our way… I did not know how to handle any of that or how to express my total appreciation for everything they were doing… What could I do… What could I possibly say… To somehow balance so much that was coming from them??? …

Nothing… Just let myself float and follow and send Love to every single one of them…

And on a Friday she emails me to say that she and the crew wanted to give my child a gift and she wanted to know if it was OK with me… And I was totally "jaw-dropped" … But more??? … What is this??? … And there was no way I could say no to so much kindness…

As I type this I remember how I was an expert at that in my "previous life" … An expert at blocking everything that was trying to reach me… Because of my rigidity… Because of my lack of self-worthiness… Because of how deeply I truly believed and was totally sure that I did not deserve anything…

And for some magical reason none of this was possible for me anymore… Even the thought of it was nowhere to be found in my mind at all… It is as if I was totally a different person… It is as if I was observing me from out of my body and could not believe what I was seeing…

There was no way I could put even the smallest barrier to what was coming to me… So much Love!!! … And now that I remember… I told her exactly that in my email… That there was no way I could say no… Not for the gift itself… Which at that point I did not know what it was… But because I could sense from the very beginning all the Love that was flowing… And overflowing from them towards us… And I knew all of that kindness came from the purest depths of their Souls…

She told me that they wanted to give a small tablet to my child… So the airport and flight journeys would be easier for me :) … And that they wanted to know which cartoons… Or which apps… I approved of… So they could download them for my child…

Could you believe this???? ... We had never had a tablet... And even though I thought it was a great idea... Going to purchase one... Or even someone giving us one would have created such stress in me at that point because I truly do not like following directions to figure out anything... I am more of a "sensing and feeling" type of person...

But this!!!! ... This was a miracle!!! ... Not only were they so thoughtful as to having the idea of getting the tablet for my child to make everything easier for us... But they went to the extreme thoughtfulness of even wanting to download things for us :) ...

And the following Sunday she calls me early in the morning... I did not hear the phone, so she emailed me... Then I called her back... Basically she wanted us to stop by... And we were out of town, so we agreed that we were stopping by on our way back, which would be pretty much at night time… She said it did not matter because she would be there all night…

When we got there several of them came out… It was a brand new tablet that they had been charging all day, so it was ready to go… They had done all the necessary set-ups for me… Gave me all the information of all the things they had set up… Had downloaded the things that my child liked… They stayed with us for a while… They just wanted to see and feel and enjoy all the happiness of my child… And my amazement…

I just wanted them to feel my appreciation and yes… My Love… I could not hold it inside of me… That feeling in my chest… It was just flowing and flowing…

And we left… And none of my relatives and friends could believe any of that…

And the day of the flight came… And my mom and my brother went with us to the airport… We had to travel to a different city… And my brother had been in many airports and many flights before… And I could see the total amazement in his face…

As soon as we entered the airport someone approached us to greet us and guide us… And took us to the next place we needed to go to… And someone there said "Oh, you are so-and-so!!!" … And they shook my child's hand… And I could tell my child was feeling extremely joyful and important… And they helped us in the process… And we sat down in the waiting area and my brother just said "This is simply unbelievable!" …

And then the time came when we had to enter to the next area… And my mom and my brother could not go there… So we had to say goodbye… And my child was very centered about everything... And I was very calmed... Then in the next room... Then at the next stage... And the next... Everyone helping us and addressing my child by name...

How did they know? ... It is clear they had been expecting us... And when we finally entered the airplane... Ohhh... My child (and me too, I have to admit) was "walking on clouds" ... They made us go in earlier... So my child could settle into it... And as we faced the entrance of the plane... The whole crew was standing there... With beautiful smiles on their faces... Waving and greeting us... And telling my child "Oh!!! ... You must be "so-and-so" ... And shaking hands and saying "Welcome, so-and-so!!!" ...

And my child was so happy... And one of the stewardesses took us to our seats... And explained many things to us... And assured me everything was going to be fine...

And as everyone else boarded the plane… And as the plane was ready to lift off… A stream of memories of all the beautiful people and circumstances that blessed us with their Love and their kindness to make sure this dream would come true kept flowing and flowing through me… And tears of appreciation and Joy and Love kept flowing and flowing from me…

And as the plane lifted I was amazed to see that even though I was expecting my child to cover the ears and be stressed out… All I could hear was the most happy "WHEEEEEEEEE!!!!!" … And I was totally delighted to see that such joyful exclamation was coming out of the happiest face I have ever seen… My child's face… Covered with a smile from forehead to jaw and from ear to ear…

That "split-second-moment" was enough for me to instantly realize that everything…

Absolutely everything that had happened in my life before... Every stress... Every effort... Every thought... Every person that crossed our paths to try to help us in one way or another... Every coincidence... Every single thing had been worth it... Just to see such an expression and such Joy in my child...

And unbelievable opportunities for learning and increase in my child's awareness popped up throughout both flights... And in every day we spent away from home... Beautiful experiences... Astonishing views...

And the day of our return arrived... And my friend and her son went with us to the airport in that 3.5-hr-away-country... And they stayed with us till the last place they could go to... And the moment to say goodbye came... And I was very calmed... And my child was incredibly well behaved...

And to be completely honest… I have to say that even though we stayed in that country only 11 days… The experience was so delightful… We visited so many places… We felt so much love in the people we met… Our emotions were so constantly on the surface of our skin… On the surface of every cell of our bodies… We Lived everything so intensely and so beautifully… That those 11 days felt as if they were truly at least a year… Everything from back home felt far away in our memory… I felt as if I had been somehow emptied out… I felt much lighter…

It was a much bigger airport than the ones we had been before… And as we were walking and following the signs to find the appropriate airline…

The thoughts about all the help we had received from all those people back home kept flowing through my mind and my body… But everything felt very distant… Like when one is daydreaming… Like floating… And we got there… And before we were able to find a place to seat… I see a lady approaching me and saying my name in the language of that 3.5-hr-away-country… A language that I know very well from having been very fluent in it in a previous stage of my life… A language that I Love so much!!!! …

And I am sure she was able to see the surprise on my face… And how puzzled I was from seeing someone approaching me by name in that language in the middle of that airport so far away from home… And she quickly explained that "that Beautiful Angel" back home had contacted her a couple of weeks ago… Explaining her about us and asking her to help us in our way back…

And I just told her how much I appreciated all of that… And how incredible this person back home was... And all the thoughtfulness... And all the Love... And how unbelievable it was that this lady in that far away country remembered to do something she was asked to do two weeks before... By someone she probably didn't even know... For two simple people that do not know anybody... That were just trying to live life in Love... And Joy... And Happiness...

And they truly helped us a great deal... Re-assigned seats to us, so my child would be in a more calmed area... And as we entered the plane... Exactly the same... The whole crew at the door... Greeting us and calling my child by name and shaking hands... And checking on us periodically throughout the flight... And making sure I was fine...

Now I realize that they all knew they needed to pay more attention to me than to my child :) ... That I was the one that was stressed out about so many things… And I am totally thankful for every one of the beautiful Angels that crossed our lives during all those months… Some for a very short time… Some stayed with us longer… But they all had a very crucial role in the completion of this wonderful dream…

And I still hear in my Soul the exclamations of my child… So many times in each flight… As the plane went a little bit up… Or a little bit down… Or all the way up… Or all the way down… And deep down inside of me I know that they were all with me and could clearly hear and rejoice in each beautiful "WHEEEEEE!!!!!!" that came out of my child's happy face… Of my child's happy Being… Deep down inside of me I KNOW that that is why they did it… Just for that beautiful moment… Just for that beautiful feeling :) … And all I can say is… Like my child usually says… "WE DID IT!!!!!!!! " …

∞ ∞ ∞

Chapter 10-- From The Universe **TO ME** And **FROM ME** To The Universe

I always felt that there was something else… Besides seeing the mountains again… Something else that "pushed" me so strongly and so fast to make that trip…

From the minute the first idea "occurred" to me… Thinking at the same time that it was something truly impossible for us to do… Like an "unrealizable dream" … To the minute we got on the second airplane to come back from our trip… With all the countless number of miracles that happened in between… And that instantaneous and undeniable "invasion of Angels" like I call it…

That "invasion of Angels" that immediately appeared in every moment of our lives those days… And caused all the possible obstacles that presented in our lives and could possibly cause this trip (dream) not to happen… To immediately dissolve…

And with the dissolving of all the possible obstacles… What totally truly dissolved was any doubt that I could have about the reality of this trip… About the reality of this dream…

There was so much help available to us! … So much help that we never requested! … So much help available from sources much… Much greater than what we could have ever imagined! … That I was totally convinced that there was something extremely deep and powerful calling us there…

Yes … We got to see my friend… Whom I had seen for the last time almost 20 years ago… And to see that it was as if we had never stopped communicating was like a miracle to me…

Yes… My child got to see real mountains… Lots of them… In a beautiful area… And a beautiful little town that looked as if it was just stuck there in a mountain… As in a fairy tale… And I got to FEEL that beautiful energy from the real mountains that I had missed so much in the last 20 years… And craved so much in the last two…

Yes… I even got to realize one of my two "major dreams" (regarding natural places) … Something that was not to be part of this trip at all… Due to how far it was from where we were staying…

But with that "invasion of Angels" in our lives… I had just to ask about it… Just for the sake of it… Out of curiosity… I had no idea where it was in relation to where we were staying… And one of those Angels (my friend) organized everything without us knowing… And it was done!!! …

We went with her family… Stayed there overnight… A 9-hour drive there… A 10-hour drive back… And it was done!... We were there!!! … And it was one of the most worth it things I have ever done!!! … We stayed in a room that had all glass walls… On the 22nd floor… And the view was magnificent!!!! … And the sensations were incredible… What a dream come true!!! … My child was totally amazed…

But nothing like going there the next morning and actually standing next to it… Such an immensity!!! … Such endlessness!!! … Such an infinity!!! ... And ripples of energy traveled and traveled incessantly throughout my body... And tears of Joy... Of admiration... Of Love... Constantly overflowed my eyes... So much beauty!!! ... Such deep appreciation!!! ... Such happiness!!! ... And just to think that not only was I being able to feel it... But that I was also being able to provide that incredible experience for my child... Was something totally breathtaking for me!!! ... **Yes!!!** ... We were standing at The Most Astonishing Waterfalls That Exist!!!!!!

But... Immense and meaningful as they are... None of these experiences compare to the Love I felt when we met a couple... 81 years old... 50 years of marriage... They were my friend's friends...

The Love I felt toward and from these Beings... The Love I sensed they felt for my child... All of that puzzled me from the beginning... It was as if we had known them forever... The next day The Wife took us to a place that deeply touched me...

And now that I think about it... We only spent with these people less than 10 hours altogether... But it was as if we had known... And Loved... Truly Loved them all our lives...

And we said goodbye to them... And from their house we headed to the airport with my friend... And all the way to the airport... And all the way to our country... And all the days after that... I could not stop that feeling inside of me... That magical feeling about these two Beings...

And I could not understand it... I had never felt anything like that... Especially something so deep... And so pure... And so beautiful... Toward two Beings we had just met... What was this? ...

And more and more happened even after we came back… Especially after we came back! … And more than a year has passed by and the deep feeling is still there… Stronger and stronger… And now I am very clear about what it is… And I am very clear that it will NEVER go away… It is Love!!!! …

The same happened to me with these two people… As to what happened to me with THAT BEING… The same spontaneity in the communication… The same spontaneity in the feelings… The same undeniability of the Love… The same build-up of energies… The same need to write… And write… The same unstoppability of the whole process when those surges of energy take place… The same manifestations in my body…

Yes... The same energies and the same need to write letters to them… And the need to send the letters to them... Without fearing or being embarrassed about whether they may think I am crazy... The same lack of guilt or shame about writing such deep and intimate things to them... Even though I have always been a very shy and introverted person...

I know very well that most people that would read those letters would think I am totally out of my mind... Because the type of things I talk about and the way they are written is not something that most people are used to...

But with these beautiful people... The same as with THAT BEING... None of it mattered... I just felt the need... More than a need... It felt almost as an "obligation" ... To make sure that whatever flowed through me about them... Would reach them... Without fear of their reaction... Without trying to stop anything from flowing...

And it really is not that I wasn't "trying" to stop anything from flowing… It truly is that I couldn't… That current that was carrying me and flowing through me and causing all kinds of strange happenings in my whole Being was infinitely much more powerful than me… It literally swept me with it… Without me being able to offer any resistance at all… Or even have the time to realize what was happening to me…

Perhaps I had to go to that 3.5-hr-Away-Country to feel all these profound things at all of those different places we visited… To feel all those profound things toward the people we interacted with…

I needed to go all the way to that country to meet these two beautiful beings… So I could then feel all this Magic for and from them… So I could realize that I was able to feel this indescribable Love towards other people and other things too…

That this Love was not something that was just limited to THAT BEING...

To be able to realize that "That Love" was a precious gift that the Universe had given me... Or perhaps it was inside of me all along... But I was totally blocking it during the first 42 years of my life...

And all of this made me able to let "That Love" flow and express itself... And feel it flowing through me... And then eventually feel it flowing to me... And let it flow... Just for me... And eventually start to write... Just for me... So I could finally Live and feel the ultimate feeling one could Live... The feeling of Self-Love... The feeling of Self-worthiness...

And the significance of this is enormous...

Thanks to what happened to me through these beautiful people… Out of the blue… I was able to realize… To bring a deeper level of clarity to the significance that THAT BEING had… And has… And will always have… In my life…

Thanks to what happened to me through these beautiful people… Out of the blue… I was able to gain deeper clarity about the significance that everything that happened in my existence in the past two years had… I gained a hugely deeper understanding about many aspects of my whole existence… Past… Present… And future…

And yes… Of course everything related to THAT BEING happened at a whole different level… And through all those intense and beautiful processes I was able to heal all the areas of my existence I already mentioned…

I was able to heal my relationship with my past... My relationship with all the people and events in my past and in my present... I was able to heal my relationship with my body... My relationship with my emotions... My relationship with mySelf... My relationship with myLove...

But honestly... I was somehow thinking and feeling that something so beautiful... So intense... So powerful... So purifying... Was a true miracle... A miracle that... If at all... Could only happen once in a lifetime...

And I feel the most blessed person in the world to have been able to Live... Even if in this "strange" way... That type of Love that somewhere deep down inside of me I knew existed... But at the same time I thought it was impossible for it to show-up and flourish in this world we live in...

So... Like I said... Thanks to all of what happened to me over the past couple of years... Especially everything in respect to THAT BEING... Now I Know that "That Love" truly exists... But I was somewhat apprehensive about the fact that I was blessed enough for me to feel it in this strange... And beautiful... And unreal way... But that it would be impossible for me to experience that ever again...

And what happened to me through these beautiful people I met in that country showed me that now my existence was... And is... In a very different stage... And that I was capable and able to experience "That Love" again... And that "That Love" that I came to know for the first time through THAT BEING... Is a type of Love very different than what we are normally used to... It is something so pure and so powerful!!! ...

My existence and the way I see life and everything around it after I met this beautiful couple is so different now… My understanding of what Love is, is so deep now… I cannot explain it… But I certainly Feel it… I Know it!!! … Love just flows… And flows… And flows…

We just need to turn "the wheel" a little… So we can turn our thoughts… Our emotions… Our Spirit… Our heart… And especially our body… Little by little… In the right direction… Just a little…

And once our body is turned just a little in the "right" direction… Like a water current… "That Love" will sweep all over and through us… As if our body was a pipe… And will "force" us completely in the "right direction"… And wash away any residues that may still remain inside of us and around us…

And the more we feel "That Love" … The more we want to feel it… And the more we carefully cultivate our thoughts… Our emotions… Our Spirituality… Our body… Like when one cultivates the most delicate and beautiful garden of the Universe…

And that becomes our only "goal" … Our only true desire... Cultivate our beautiful existence in such a way that more… And more… And more Love can inundate us… And flow from us… And to us… And through us… To everything and everyone… And flow… And flow… And flow…

And when we reach that point… We have received the greatest blessing… The blessing of Self-Unconditional-Eternal-Infinite-Unstoppable-All-encompassing-Pure… LOVE…

Chapter 11-- WHERE TO Now???

I would like to take credit for all of this... For all the transformations in my Being... For all the transformations in my body... For all the transformations in my personality... In my spirituality... In my happiness... In my Love... And for having the willpower... For having the vision of the "right way" my life needs to follow... But I can't... It was not me... All of this was "done to me" ...

But... Thinking about it... Yes!!!! ... I do need to take full credit for it! ... For the fact that at some point I was able to let go and TRUST... And had the patience to closely monitor my thoughts and emotions... And twist them just a little at a time… And many… Many times… When I wasn't successful… I did not give up on that TRUST…

Probably for the first time in my life there is something I have not given up on… It is as if even when I had given up on pretty much everything… There was something very underlying… Very hidden… Impossible for me to clearly feel it… But present enough for me to somehow sense it… Even if at what it seemed to be an unconscious level… Somehow I sensed that in no way I should let myself go further down… And endured all this without fear…

Yes… The most amazing thing to me was that I was able to endure all this without fear… Perhaps fear of failure… Perhaps that fear of failure is what has caused me to give up on everything I have given up in my life… Or perhaps the lack of self-worth… Or perhaps… Or perhaps… I do not know… All of that is occurring to me as I type this… The fact is that this is the first time in my life that "that perhaps" is not present…

It is as if an inside current that is almost imperceptible… But at the same time is very constant… And very strong… That imperceptible and strong inside current is carrying me through all of this… Knowing exactly when to speed up… When to slow down… When to pretend it is not there… So my negativity at times does not make me fight against it… No fear… Perhaps for the first time ever…

Or perhaps that imperceptible and strong inside current was always present in my life… Alongside with the fear of failure… And it was all part of a beautiful process of learning and Love… Perhaps… Who knows??? …

At this point in my life… June 9, 2015… I can say without a doubt that seeing the huge progress I've gone through within mySelf… The excitement of continuing to grow within mySelf… And to feel so good as I have been feeling for the past two years… All of that is much more fulfilling and joyful than anything "material" I have achieved before… Even though I deeply love the material world too… But the "material world" comes and goes and many times transforms itself into a source of burden and stress…

But once you experience "this"… And you know how to go back to it again and again… It is yours forever… And it is an eternal source of Joy… Bliss… And Love…

Since the very beginning… While going through the deep confusion that all of these intense processes were causing in me… Even then I could sense… As I explained before… That it was good... That all of it was part of some type of healing that was happening to me... Now I don't just sense it... I Know it!!! ...

After going through this so many times... Experiencing all these physical transformations... All these changes... Actually feelable and visible in my body... I Know this process brings some type of healing... To my physical body... To my mind... To my emotions... To my personality... To the way I remember the people and events throughout my life... To the meaning and the significance that it all has had in me... To my Whole Being... To my Whole Life...

And I feel only Love... And I Know it is all about Love... And I Know Love is the only thing that exists... Love is our only Truth...

I will be for all eternity thankful for THAT BEING's "sudden"... And abrupt... And powerful… And unignorable presence in my life… THAT BEING helped me to know me… To truly know me… To completely know who I AM… For the very first time…

As I type this… Ripples of goose bumps travel all over my skin… THAT BEING helped me to become stronger… To make my happiness depend only on me… To feel… For the first time ever… What I now know… Without a doubt… Is Unconditional Love…

THAT BEING helped me to bring clarity into my life… Every time THAT BEING did something I did not like… I turned into me… Turned the wheel a little bit… And found Love inside of me… And more Love… And more Love…

Now I realize that "all" that THAT BEING helped me to do was to focus… All that those two beautiful people that I met in that "3.5-hr-Away Country" helped me to do was to focus... All that my child helped me to do was to focus...

And then from there I drew in feelings... Thoughts... Knowings...

I can feel now the huge importance these people have had in my existence...

My existence has been similar to a water that has been running everywhere... Flooding... Inundating everything on its way... Especially my Self... Then these people... In this very crucial and pivotal moment in my life... Have had the extremely important function of helping me to focus in a very powerful way... A function very similar to that of a pipe or a canal... That pipe or canal is able to guide the water through a specific... A very defined path... Then that water can accomplish a meaningful function… Then that water has a very beautiful purpose…

At the moment all this was happening… I had no clue of what was happening with me… All I could do was try to survive the intense processes… The intense feelings… The intense sensations… The intense energies… Just trying to hold on…

Yes… These people's presence in this very crucial moment of my life helped me to focus… To act like a pipe or a canal to "force" my existence to go through a very meaningful path… A very specific and narrow and defined path to accomplish a very meaningful purpose… The most meaningful purpose of all my existence…

The purpose of changing me… Or… Better yet… The purpose of helping me to remember who I was… The purpose of Knowing who I truly

AM... For the very first time... The purpose of getting to know the greatest and deepest Love of all... Self-Love... For the very first time... In such a beautiful... Powerful way... That I know it will never go away...

This time I know I will never forget... Ever again... Who I Am... My true essence... Love...

And I know... I will ALWAYS Love Them... Very intensely... Very deeply... Very profoundly...

And I know... I will ALWAYS Love Me... Very intensely... Very deeply... Very profoundly...

With this Love that through them inundated my Being... With this Love that through them filled up my Being... And from there overflew...

It overflew... And overflows... Everywhere... Everywhere I go... To everything I see... To everyone I know... In everything I feel... To everything I touch... To everything I think about... And back to me... And from me to them... Directly to them... Always to them...

But this time there is no need of a pipe or a canal... Love does not need that... Love does not need anything that guides it or makes it go or be one way or another... Love just is... It is the only thing we truly need to realize in our lives...

And once we open ourSelves to it... There is no need for any pipes ever again... Everything has a purpose... Everything has a meaning... Wherever it flows... Wherever life takes us... Everything is magical... Everything is a blessing...

So… If someone ever asks me: What is the greatest blessing of your life? … I… Without a doubt will say: "All of it!!! … Every moment… Every event… Every person… Every feeling… Every action… Every thought… Every emotion… Every energy :) … All of it!!! … LIFE!!!" …

11:11-- Epilogue

www.ingramcontent.com/pod-product-compliance
Lightning Source LLC
Chambersburg PA
CBHW022357040426

42450CB00005B/226